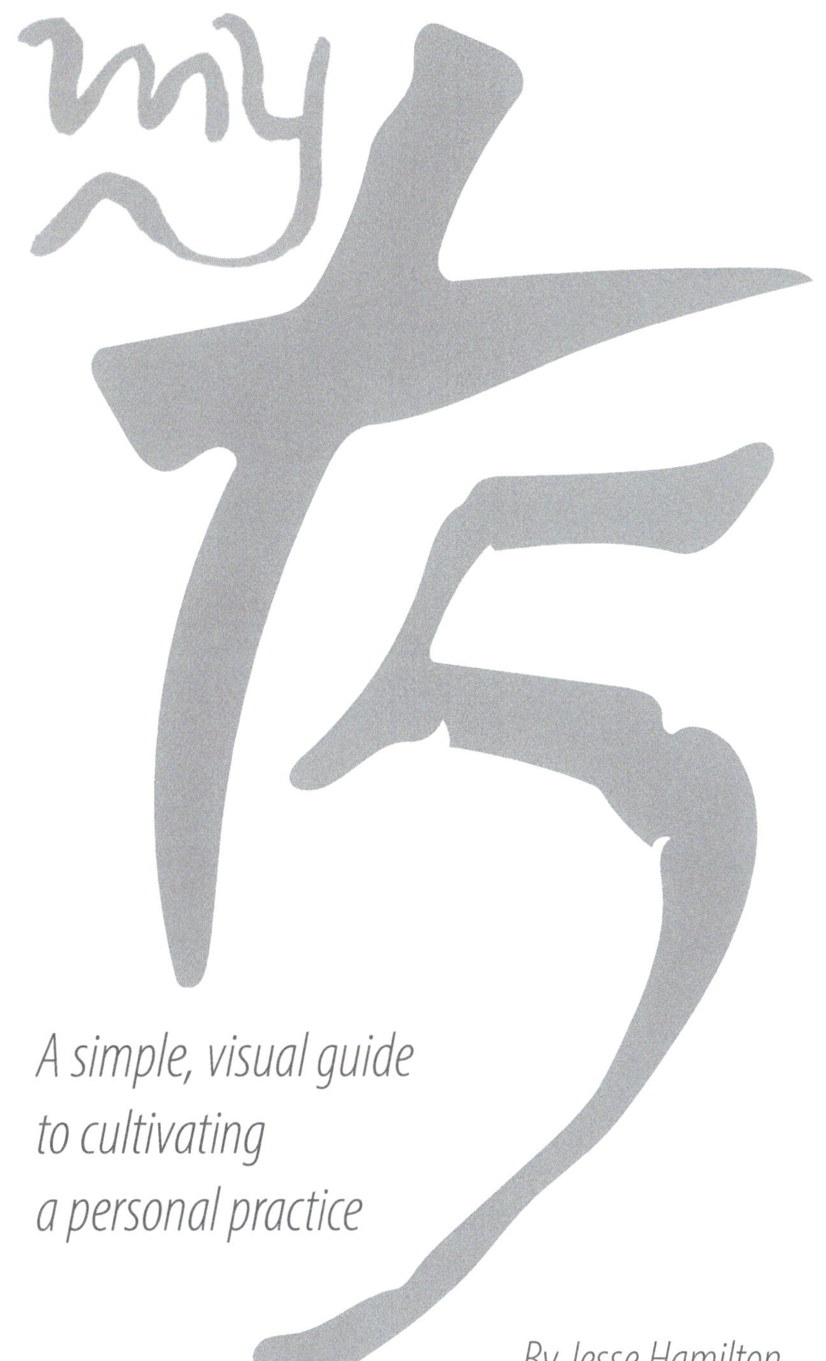

*A simple, visual guide
to cultivating
a personal practice*

*By Jesse Hamilton
Artwork by Melissa Lofton*

Change is the only constant

CONTENTS

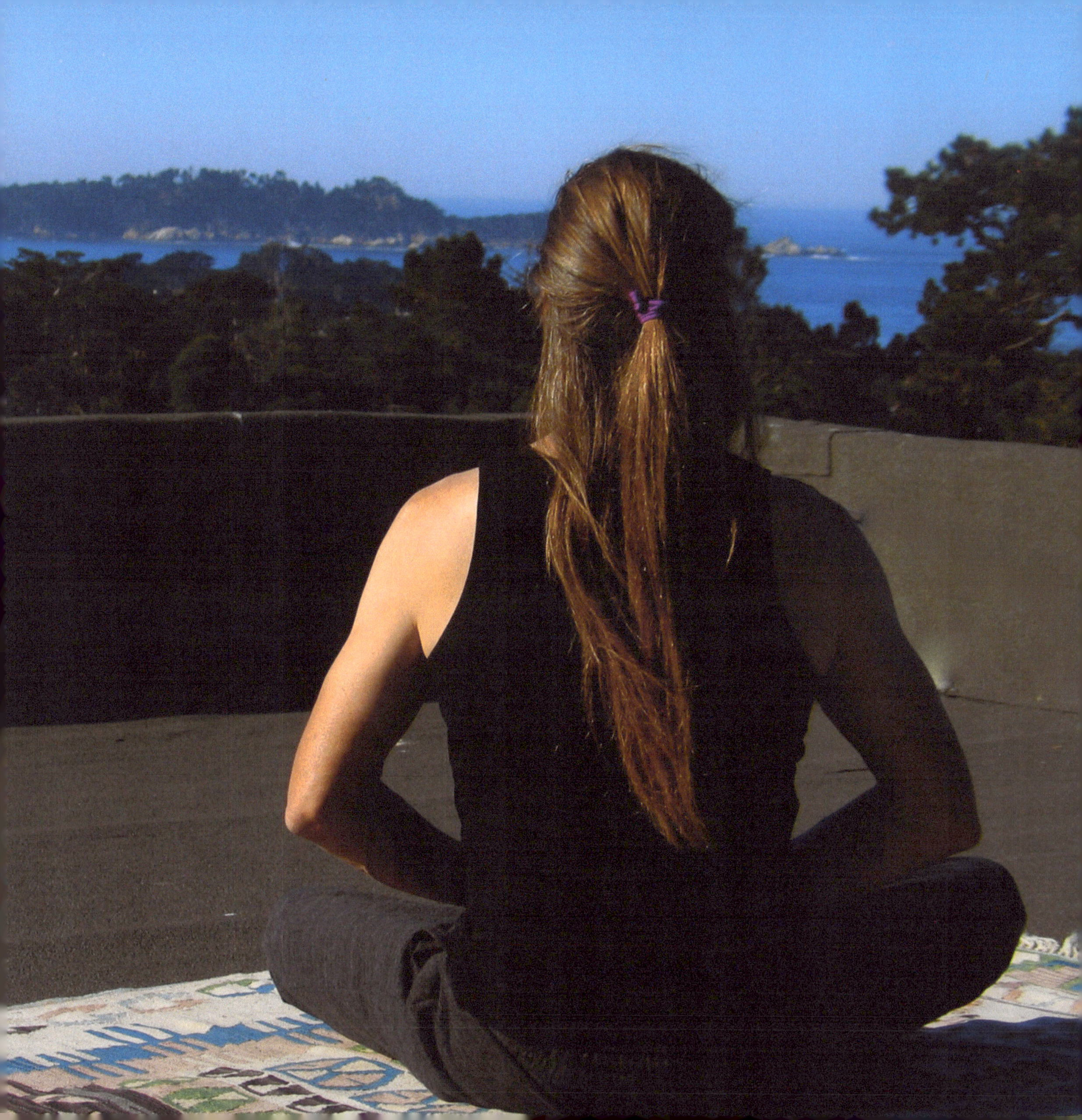

CHANGES

*This book was written, and all the photographs taken, over a period of time
when we were living on Green Ridge above the Palo Colorado watershed on the
California coast. I moved there in 1986 and Jesse in 2015. We poured all of our
energy and creativity into making a verdant, unique and beautiful place to be.
It was a haven and retreat for us and for all who came to visit.*

*On July 22nd, 2016 the Soberanes Fire roared through and, in a matter of hours,
our house, studios, greenhouses, gardens - all that you see in the following pages
- were destroyed.*

*In a heartbeat, MyT5 took on a whole new significance. The book was nearly
ready to print and we had only the forward to write, which we were awaiting
insight to complete. The Taoist principle of change has been made evident in
undeniable ways, and now we are faced with a whole new set of life-puzzles.
Our life, though entirely different as sort of refugees, has a few constants: Jesse
does the T5 most mornings, albeit on a different roof, and the creativity flows
in a slightly altered direction. We will build a new home, following the example
of the plants and trees in our garden, which within a week had started to send
up green shoots with astonishing vigor. Though it will not be the same lovely
place it was, our home will be another lovely, nurturing, inspiring haven for all
who come to be there. Through our efforts, the help of numerous friends and
neighbors and the generosity of many people, a whole new, as yet unknown,
place will be born and grow.*

*Melissa Lofton
October 9th 2016*

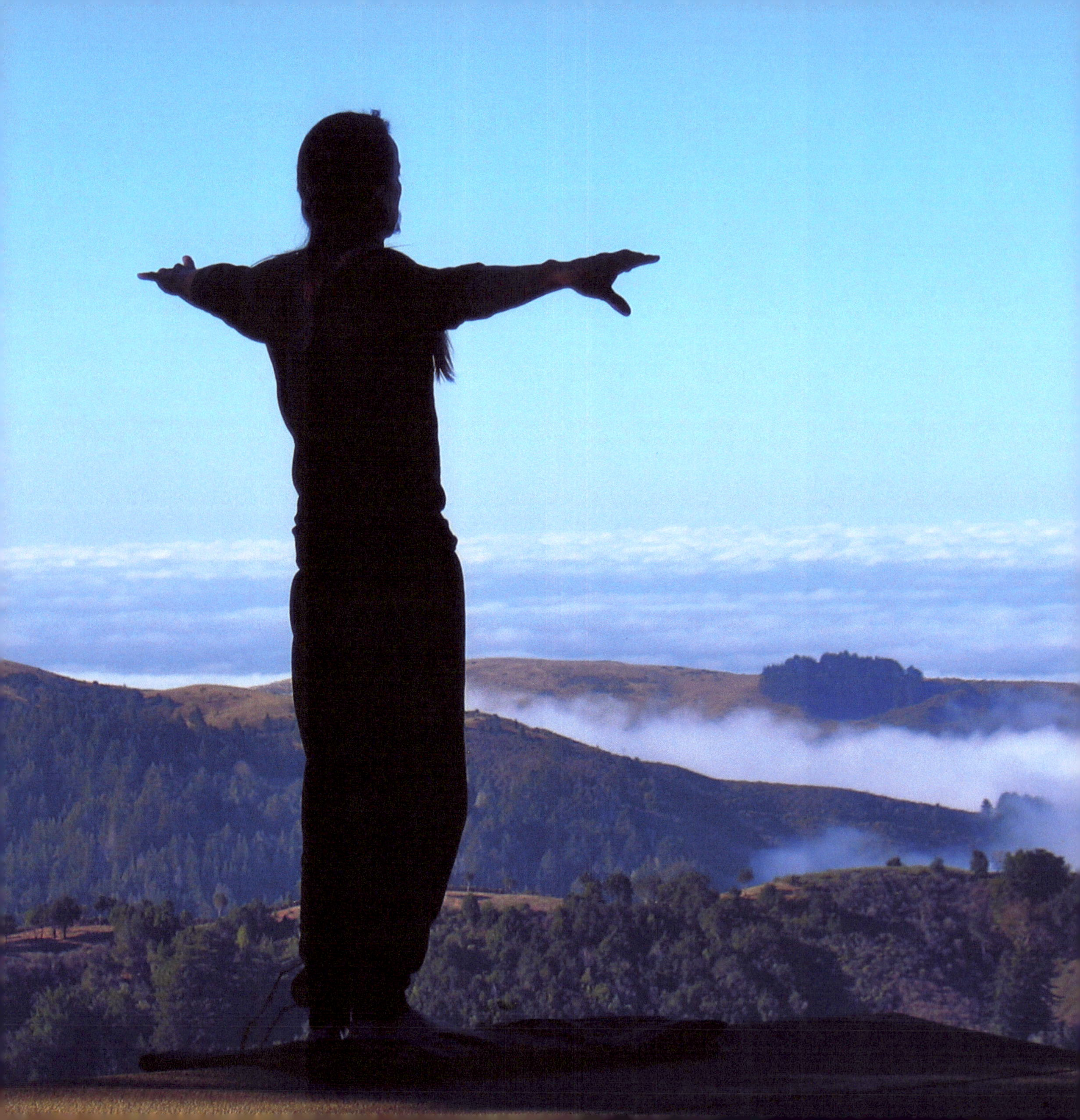

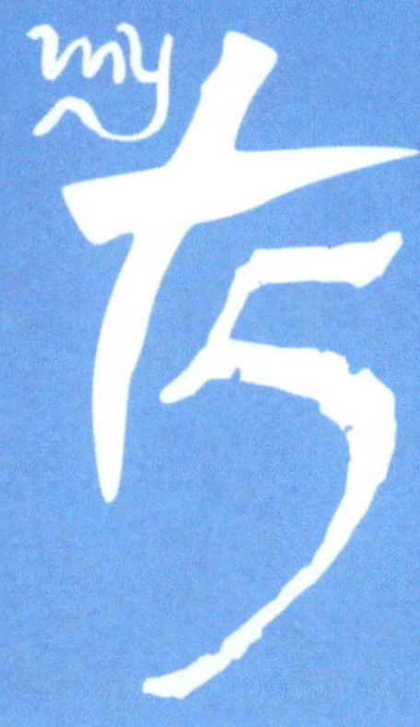

This is my experience with the Five Tibetan Rituals. When I came across them, I realized immediately that this was what I was looking for: five simple, easy to remember and graceful, efficient movements.

With this information, I started my own practice, developing the movements you find in the following pages.

JH
2016

Moving at the speed of breath, with the exception of twirling, where you count the revolutions you make, each movement is made with breathing: one inhale, one exhale, one movement.

*All movements are transitions,
breathing from one place to another,
21 times.*

A strong focus is required for counting.
Soon the movements will be easy for you and
stopping at 21 becomes necessary to avoid
wasting energy or creating fatigue.

It is simple to develop a lifelong practice
because the practice adapts to our constantly
changing body. It is a continual physical therapy,
building a structure to eliminate or avoid future
injuries or blockages through a sound practice.

my

5

5 Simple
Movements

21 times

Enter Spinning

Elevated Soles

Sunning Roc

Upward Ox

Stretching Dog

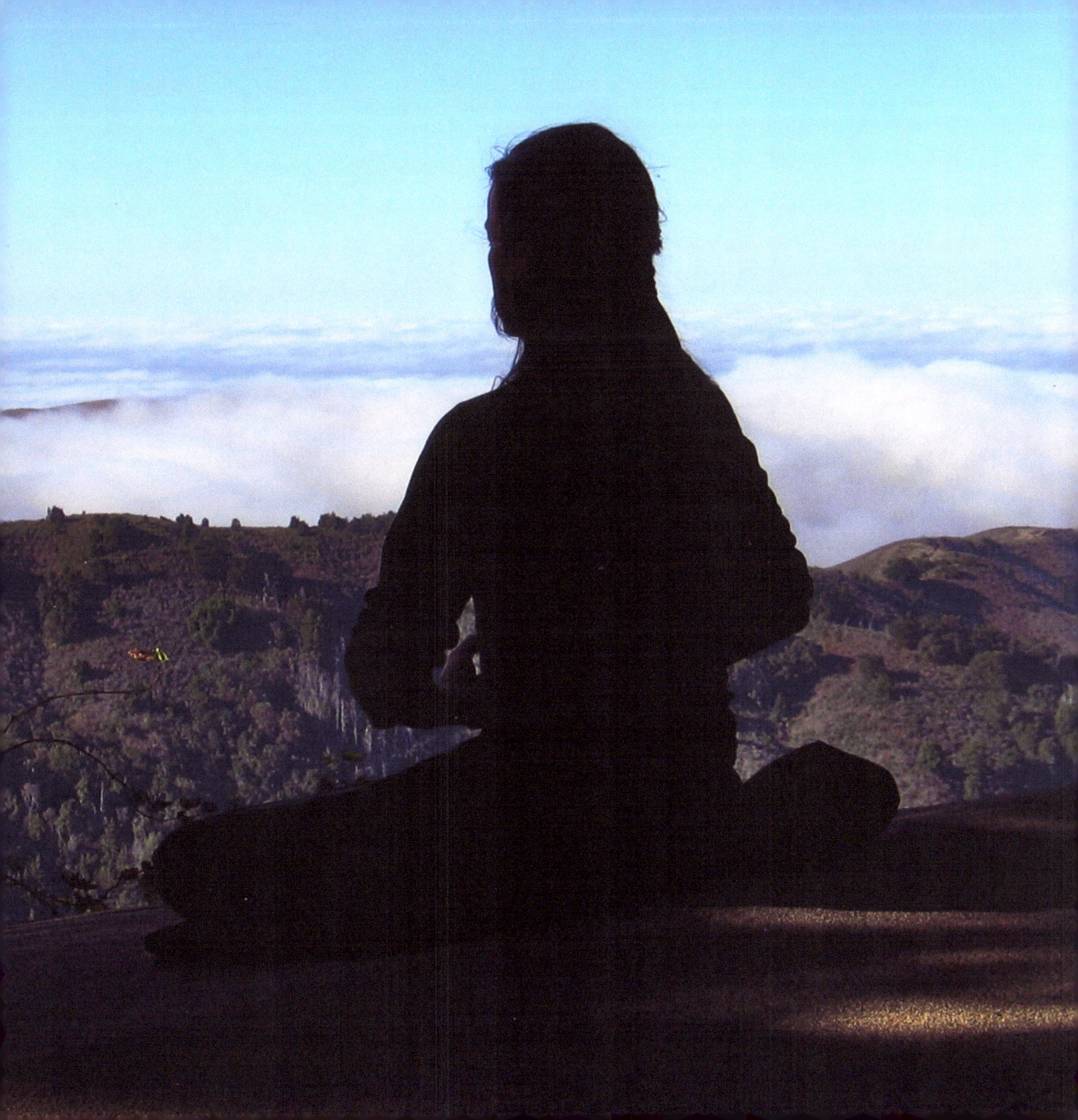

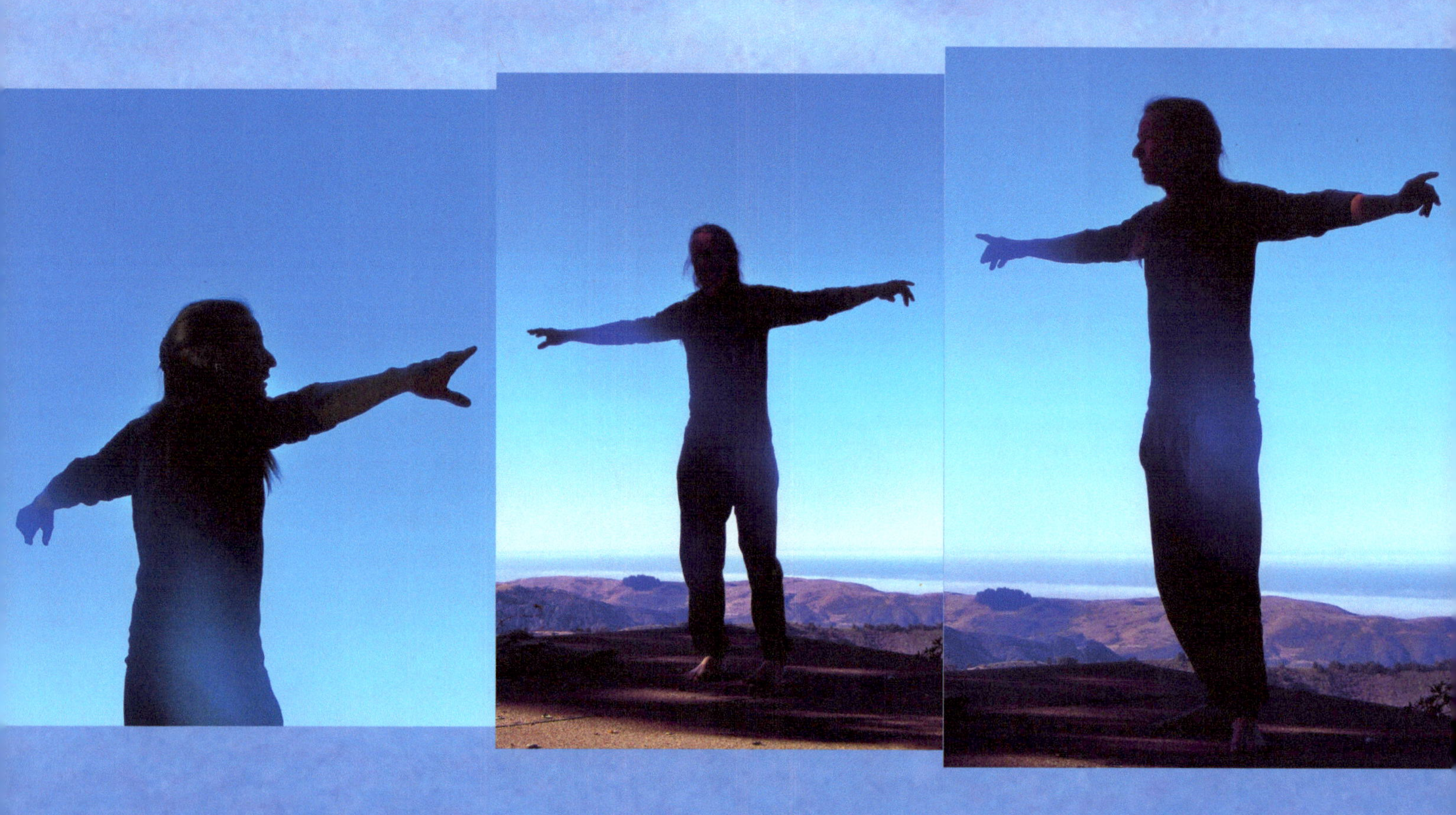

Enter Spinning

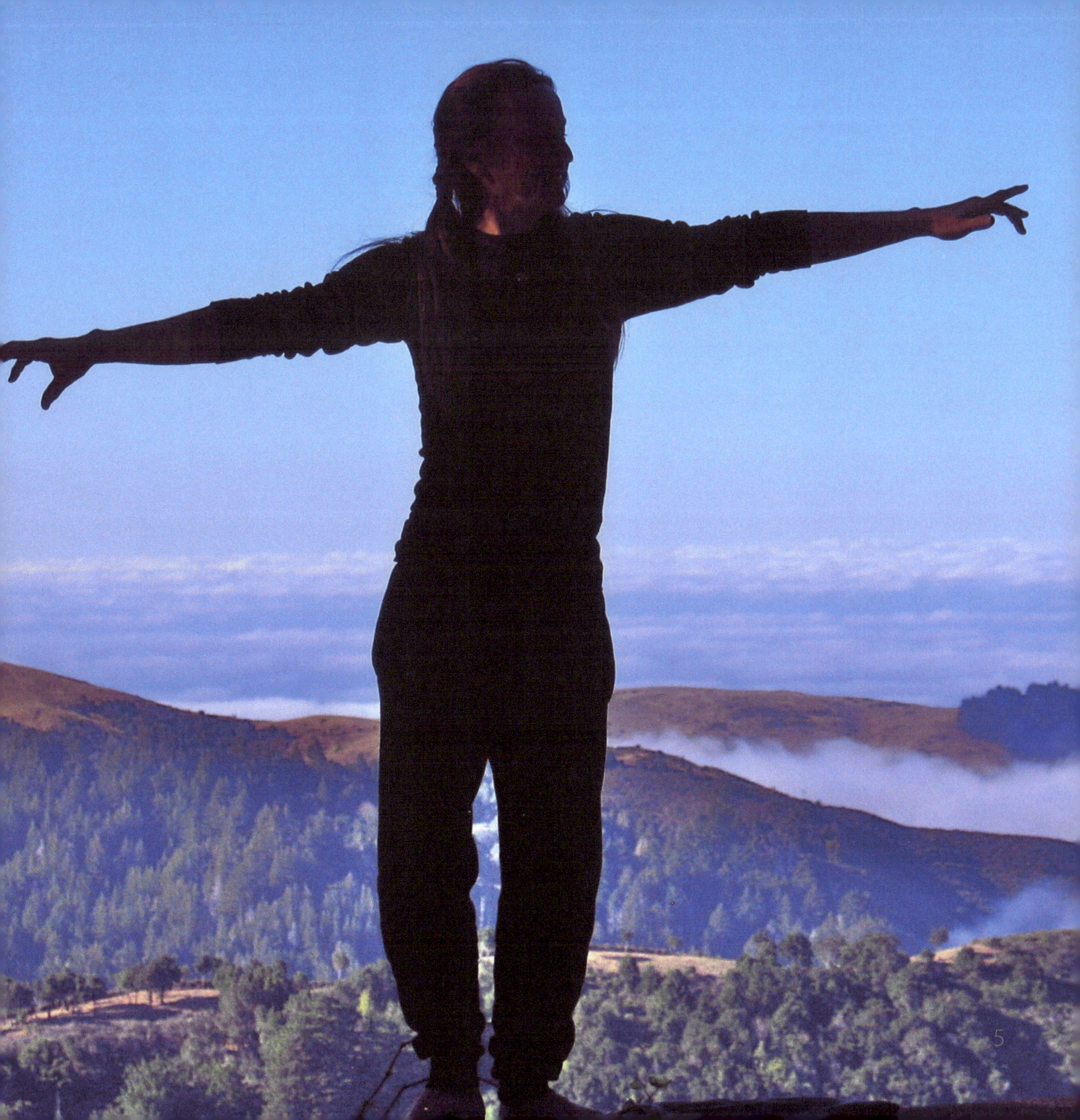

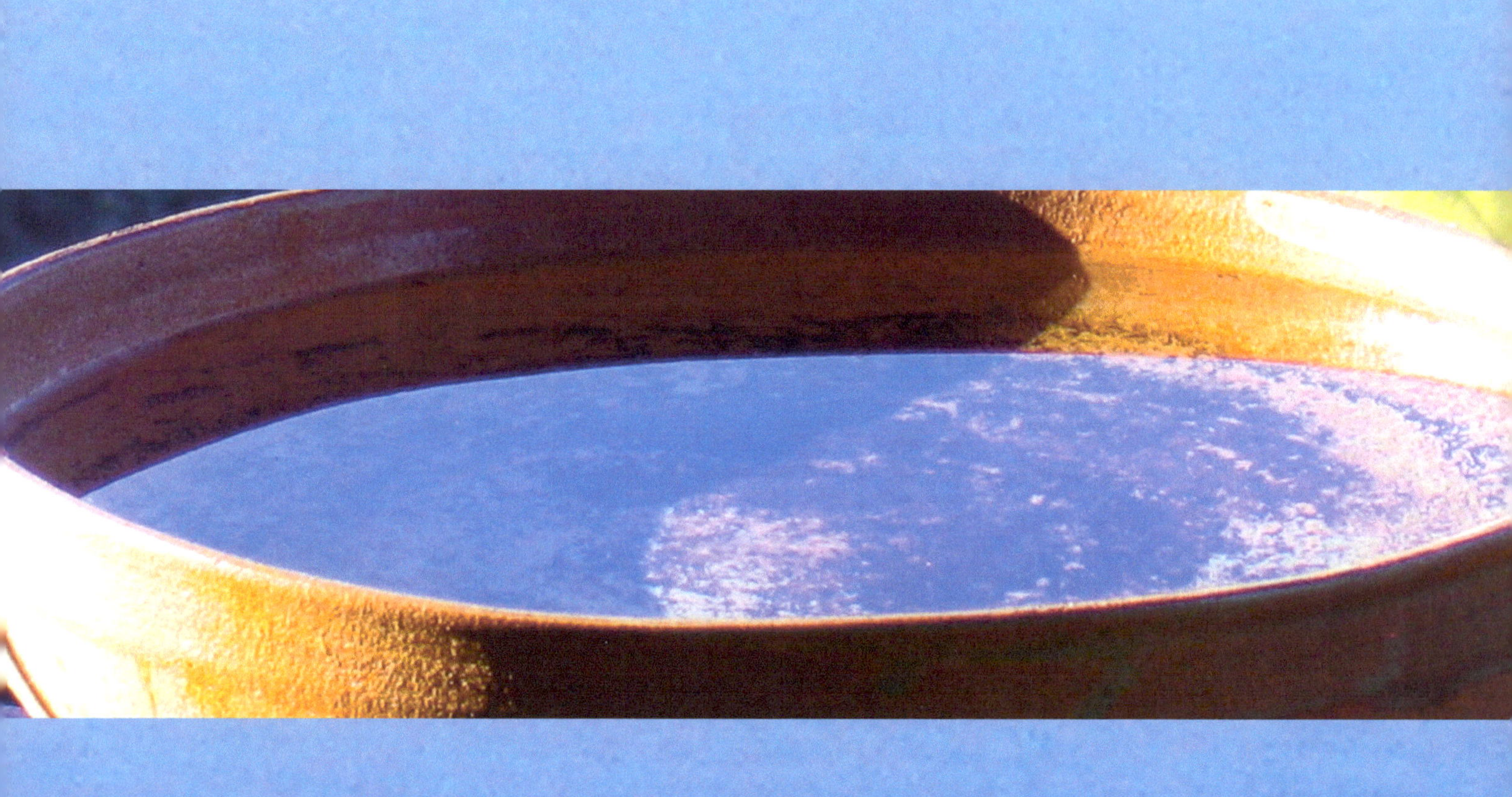

Containing

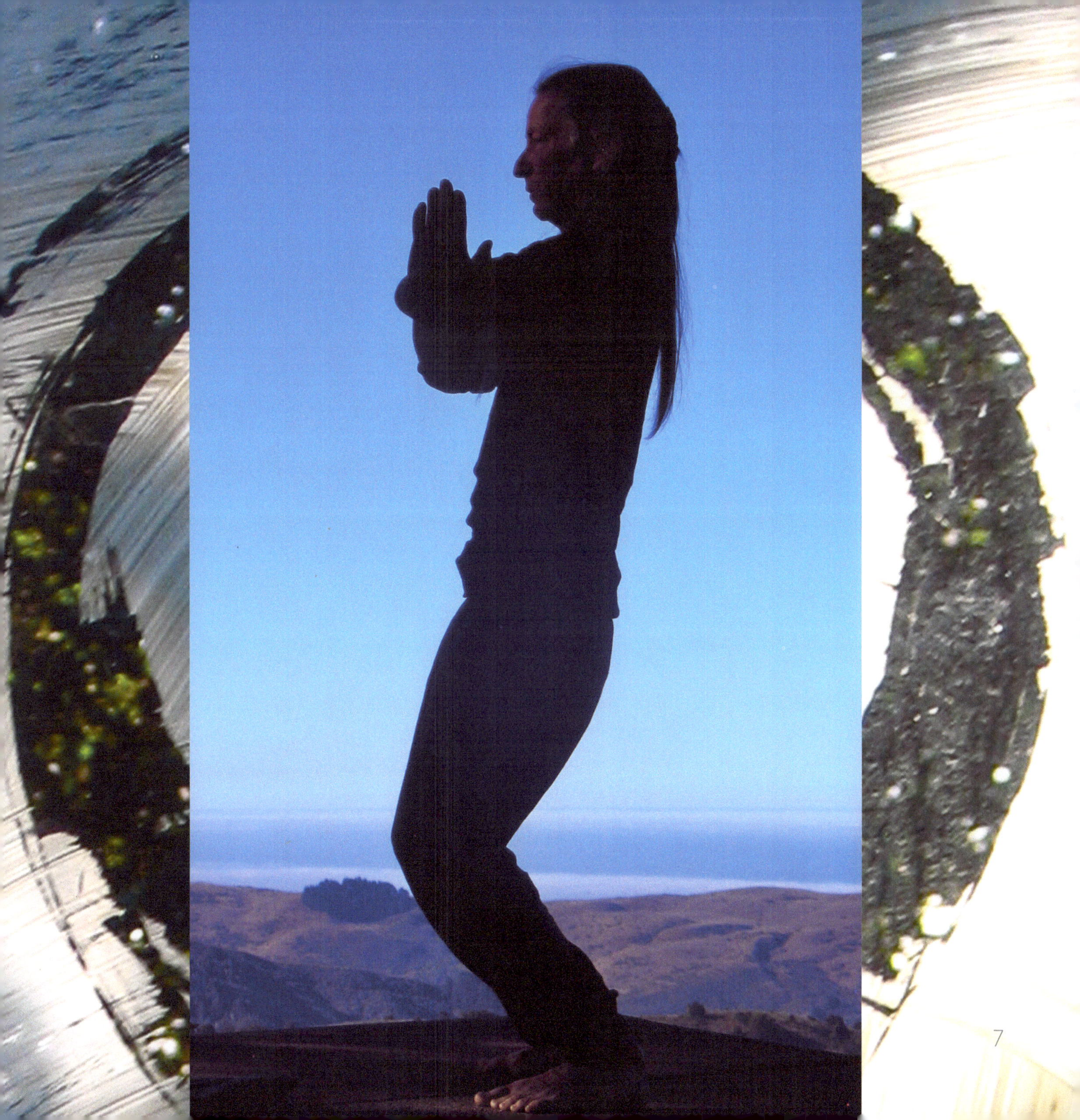

Enter Spinning / Containing

Turning clockwise, counting revolutions, arms outstretched, hands open, moving slowly, fingers stretching. Eyes seeing everything.

Ending at 21, facing the most pleasing direction, inhaling, bringing hands together, arms straight.

Exhaling, drawing hands toward face, elbows raised, bending knees together. Focusing inward.

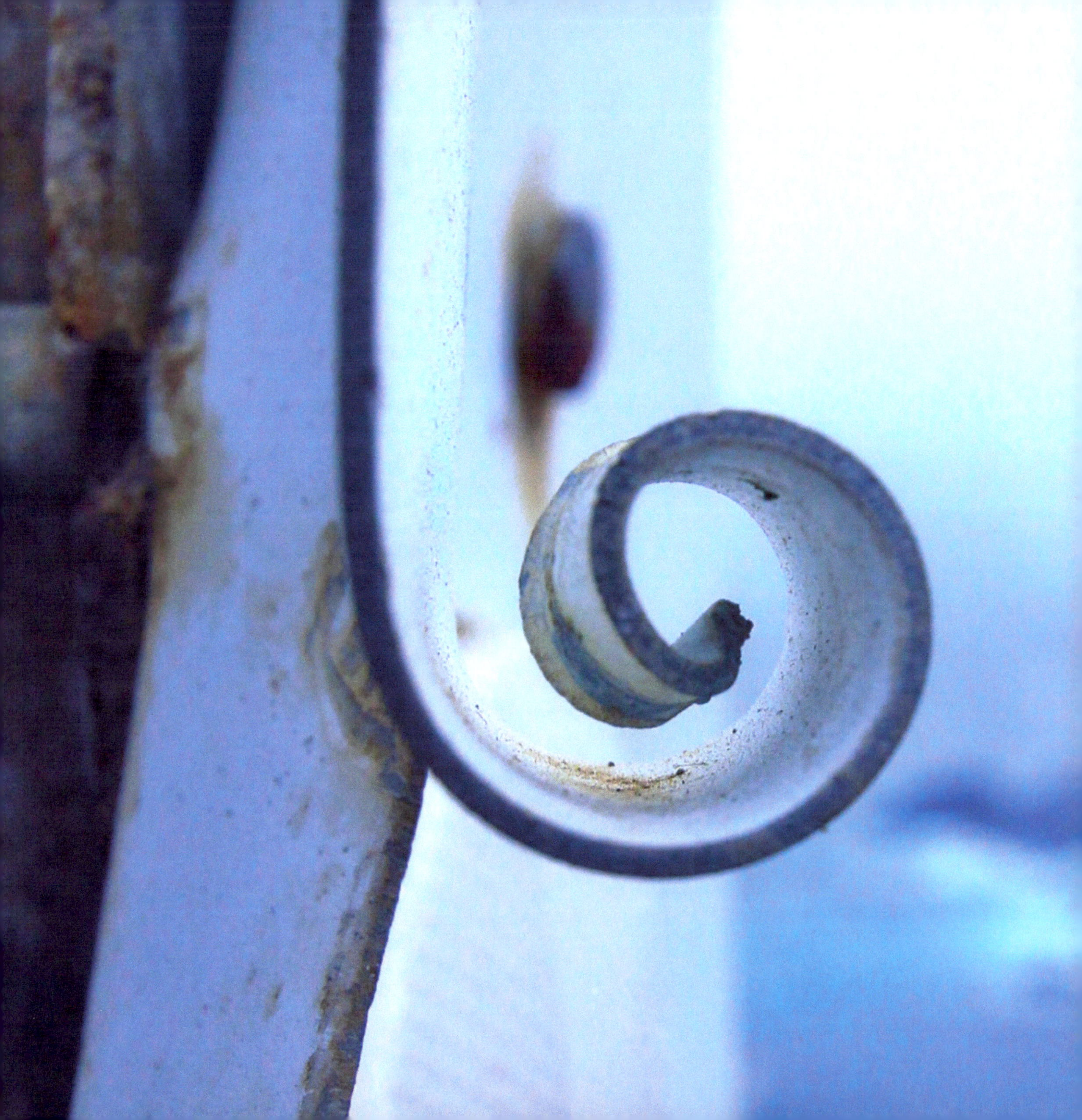

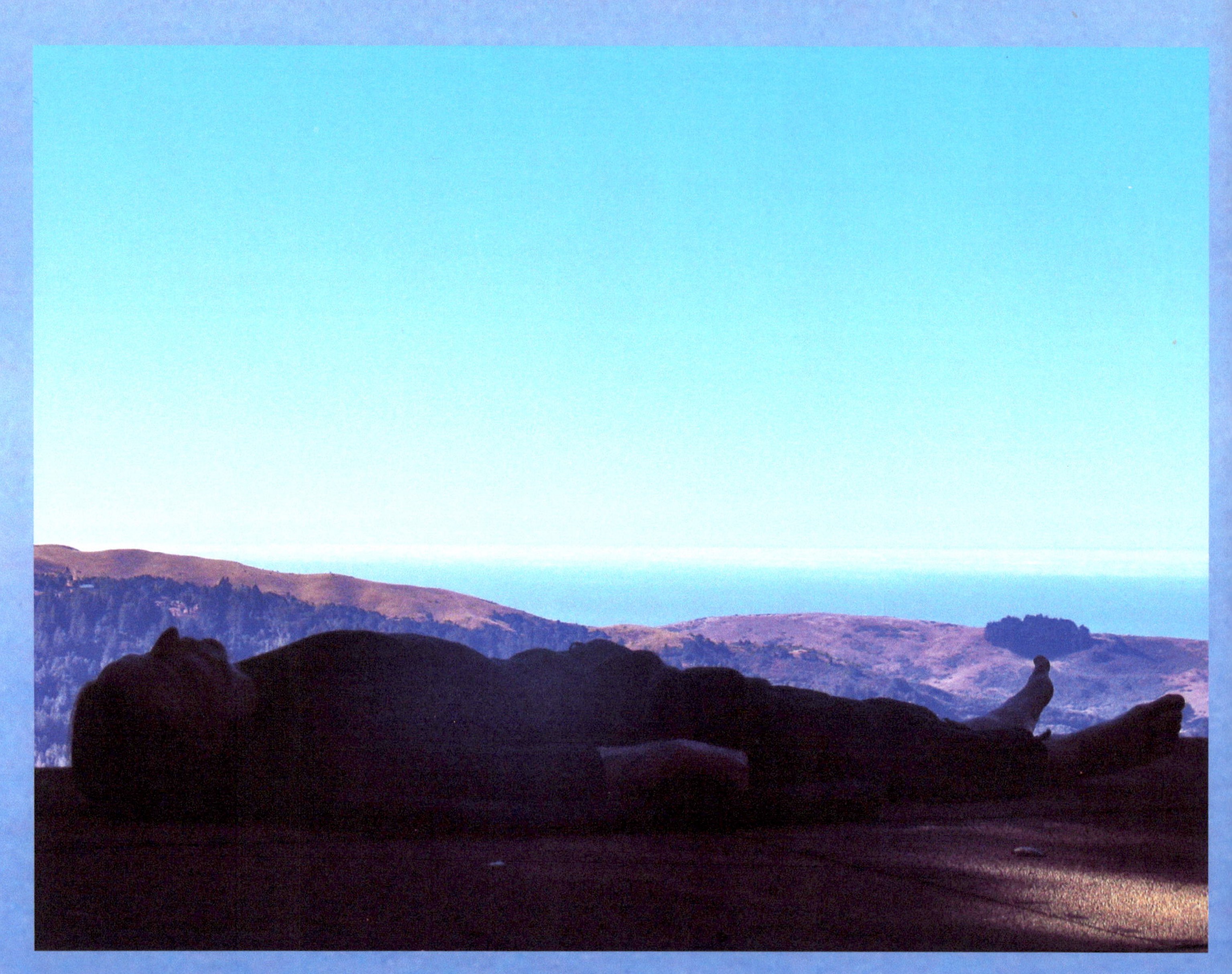

Elevated Soles

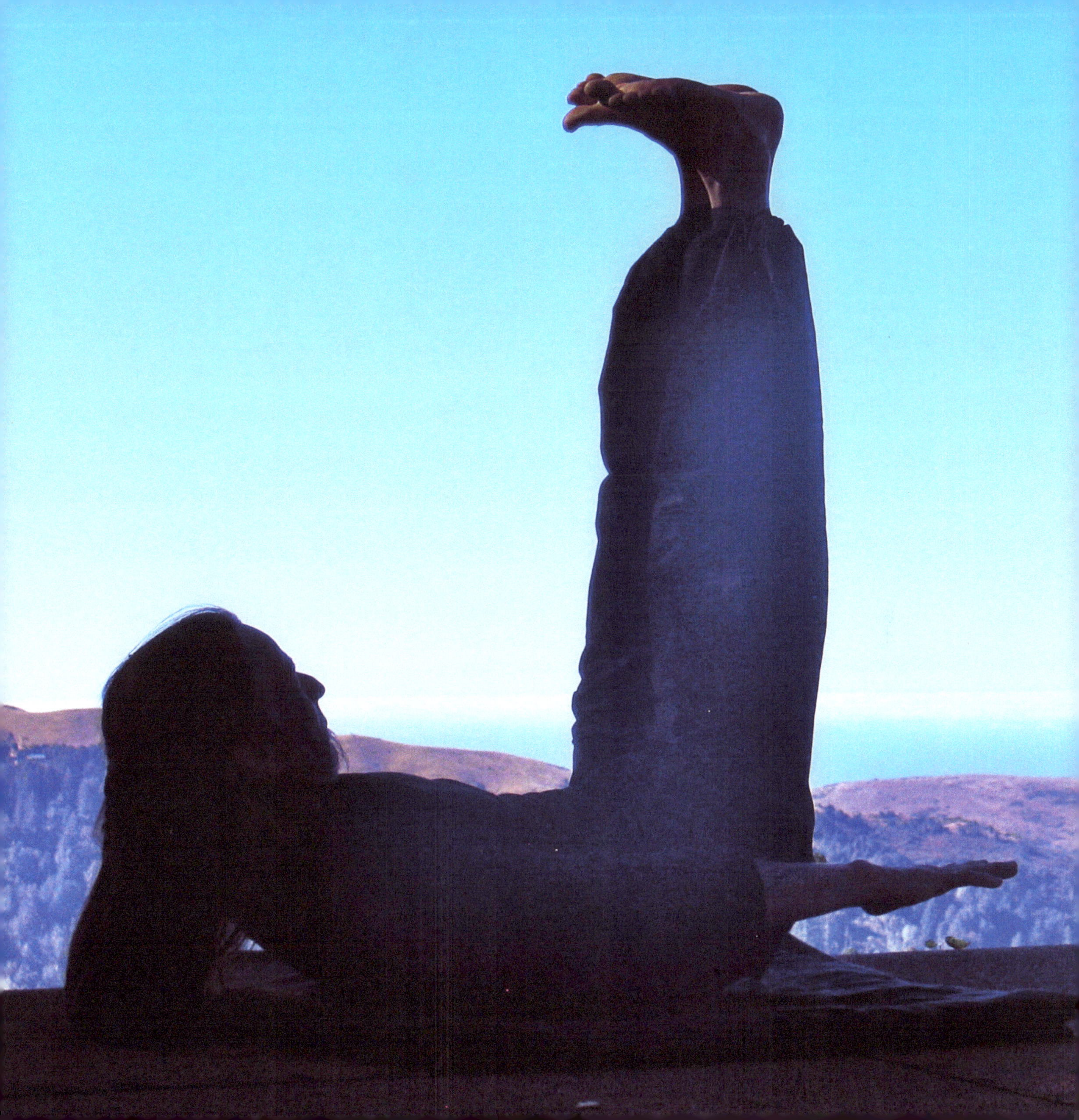

Elevated Soles

Lying on back, comfortable and relaxed, hands closed, palms down, nose to sky.

Inhaling, raising head and legs at the same time, rolling shoulders forward, raising open hands a few inches, palms down, arms straight at sides. Hold briefly.

Exhaling, lowering head and legs slowly, rolling shoulders backward, closing hands, palms down.

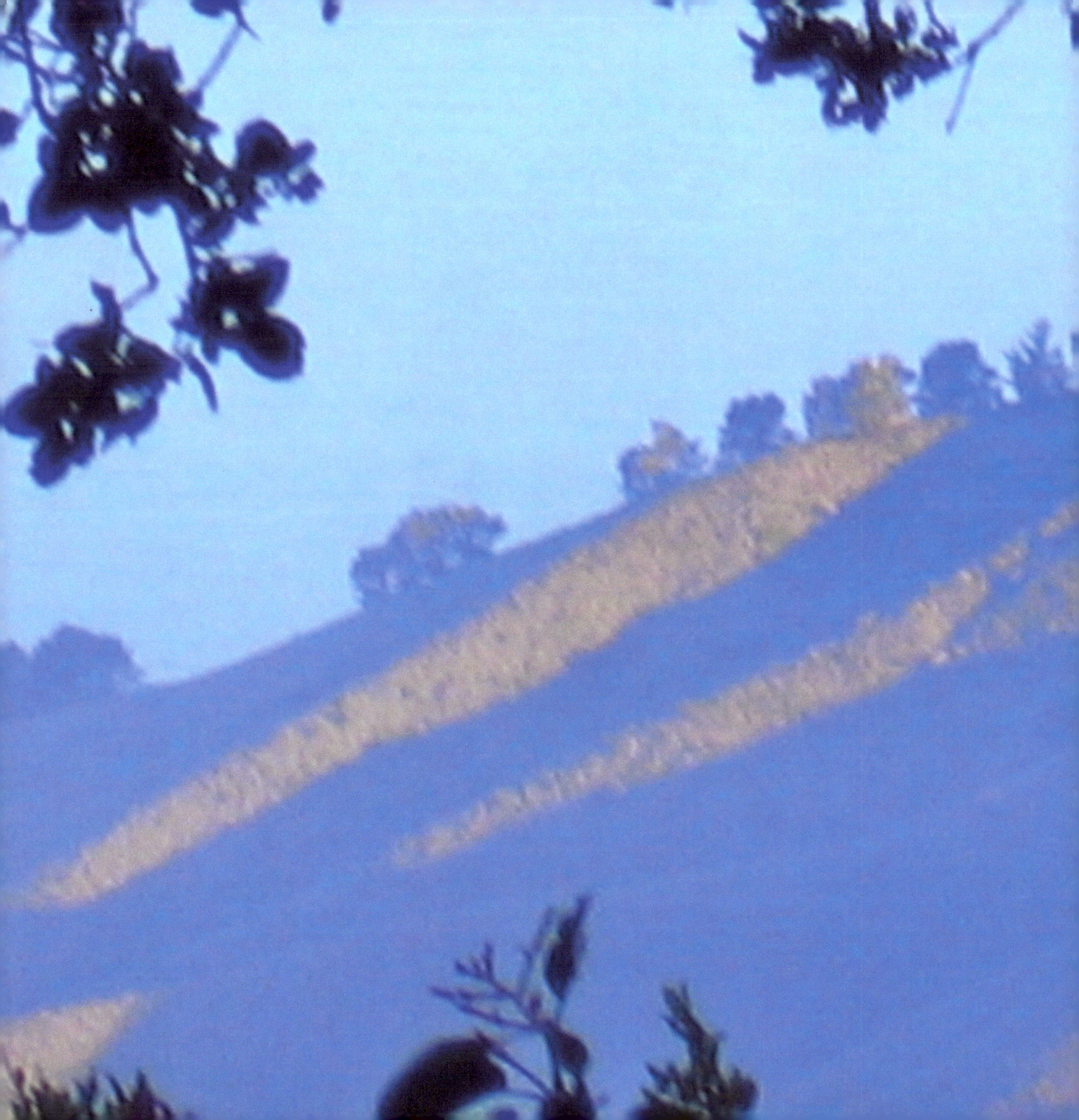

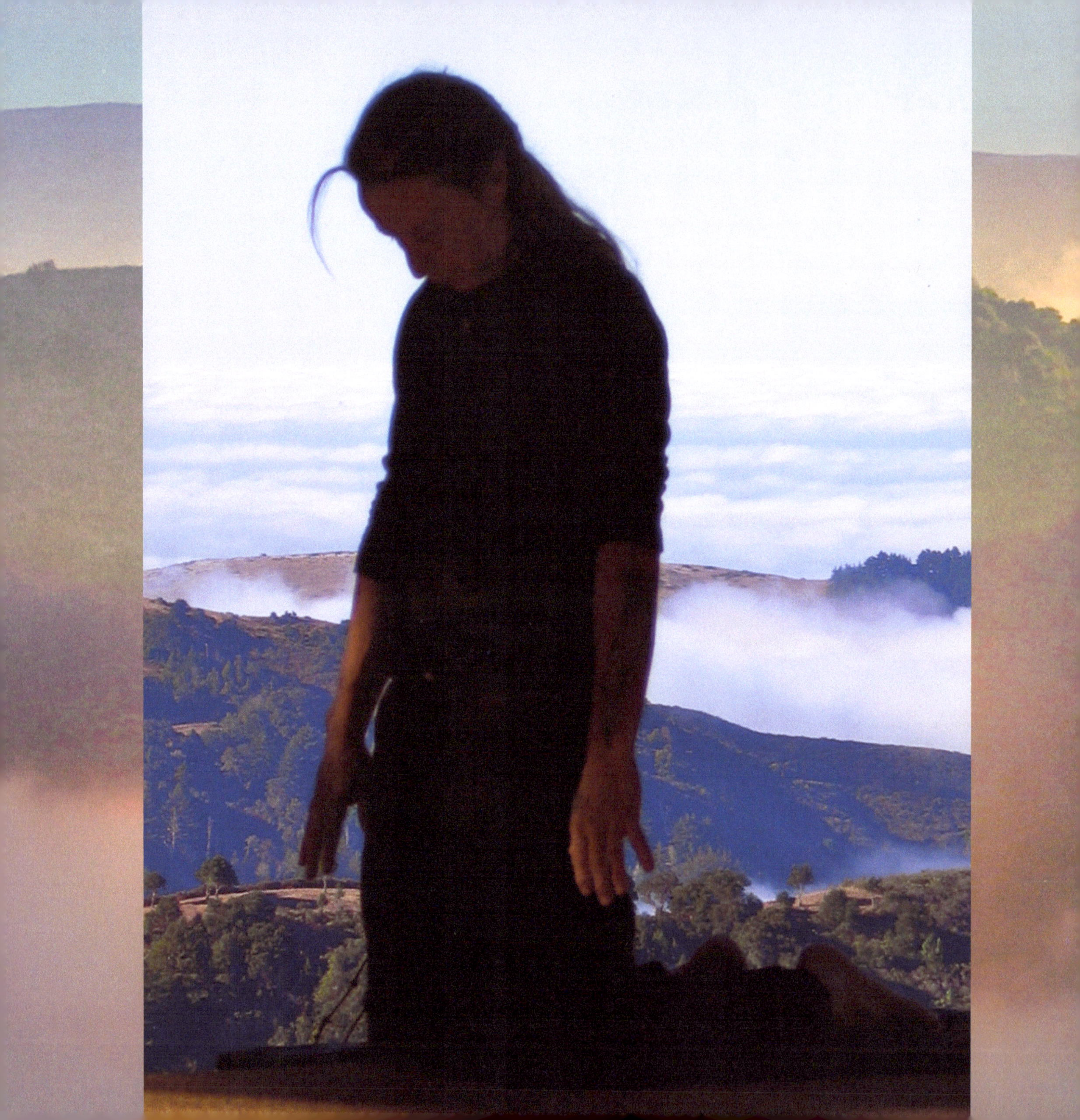

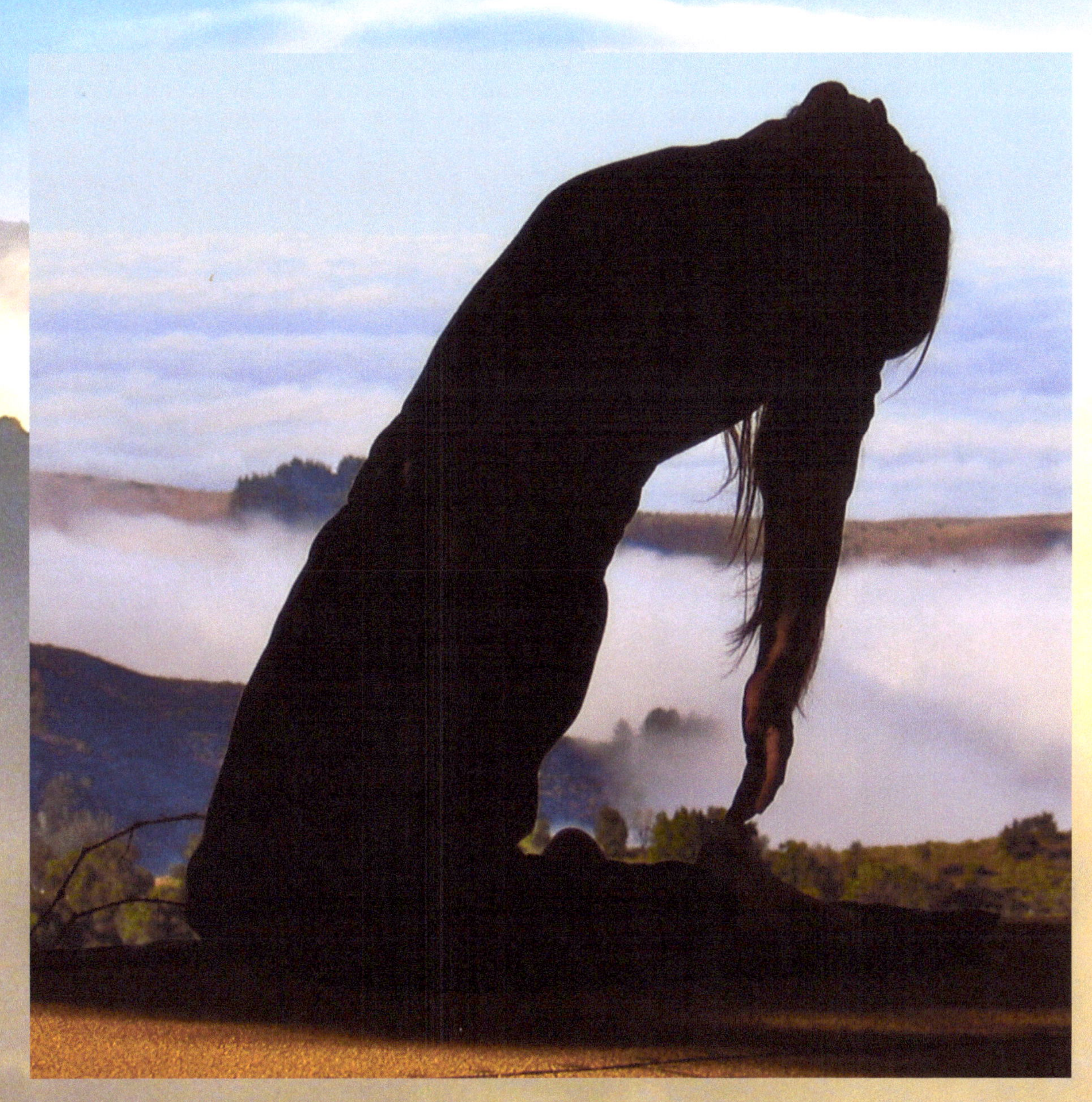

Sunning Roc

Sunning Roc

Kneeling, weight over knees, chin to chest, hands open, palms facing back.

Inhaling while rolling shoulders upward and outward, hands rotating back, palms facing forward, head leaning comfortably back. Holding for a moment.

Exhaling, shoulders rolling forward, palms facing backward again, chin to chest.

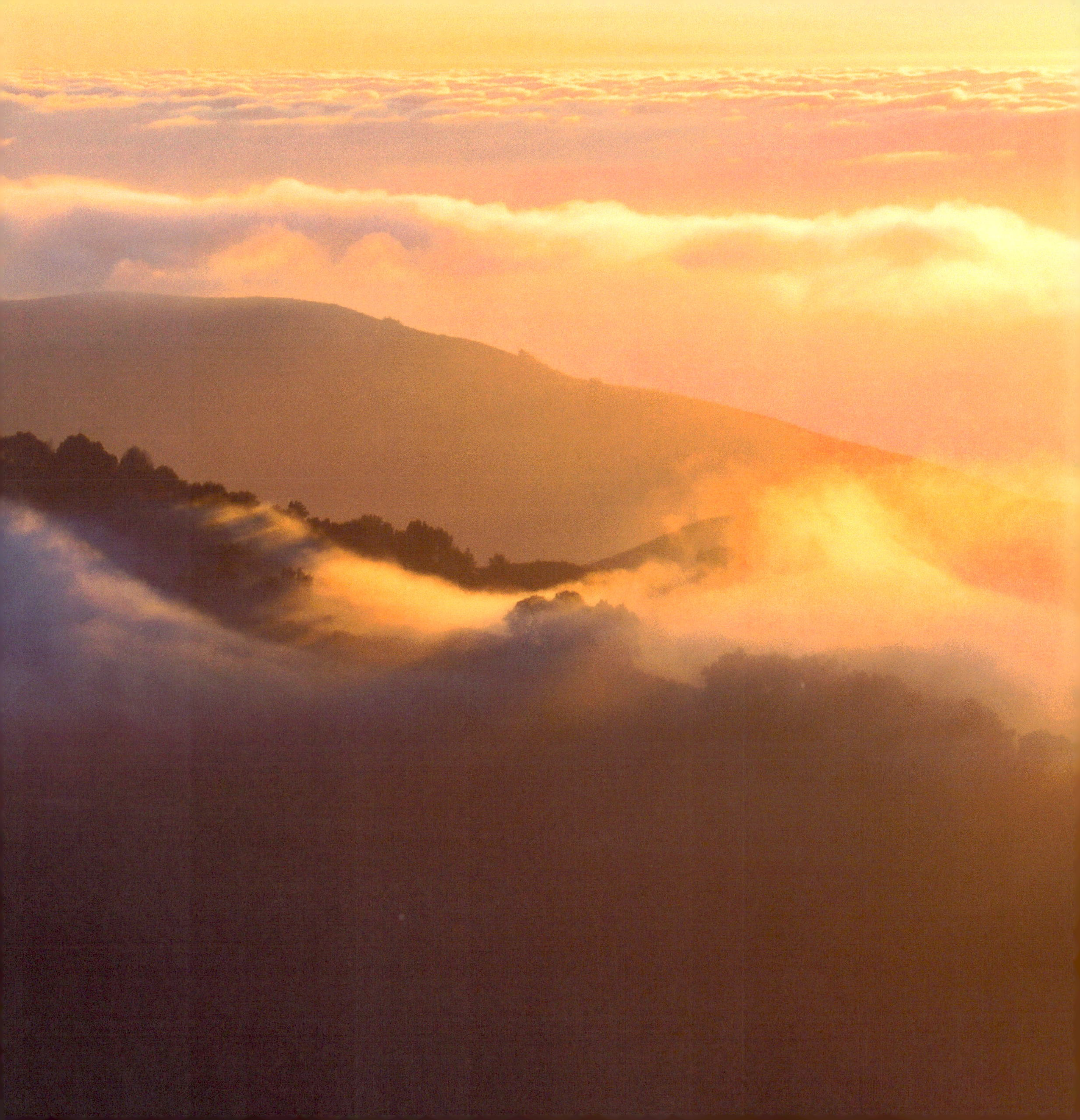

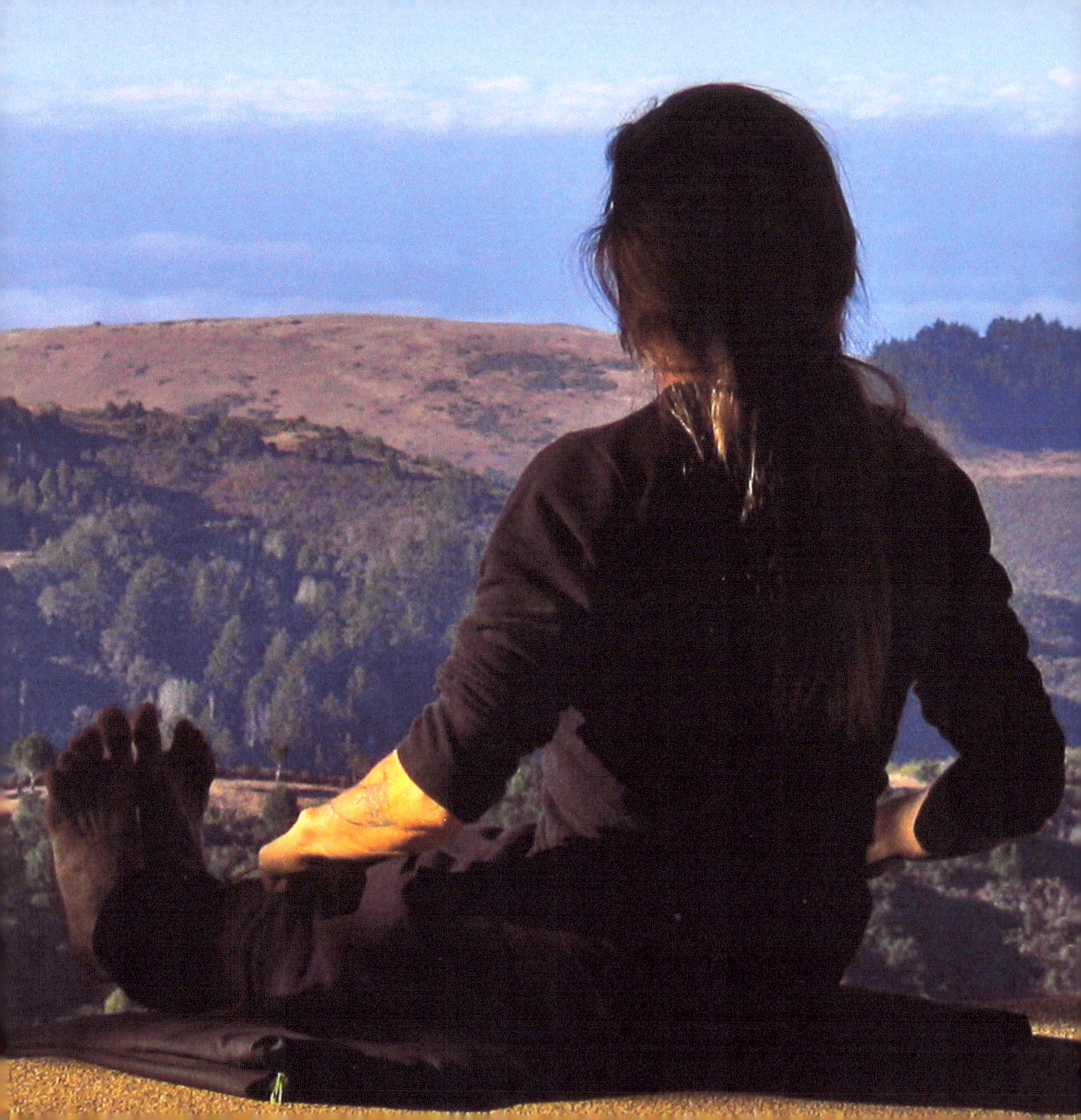

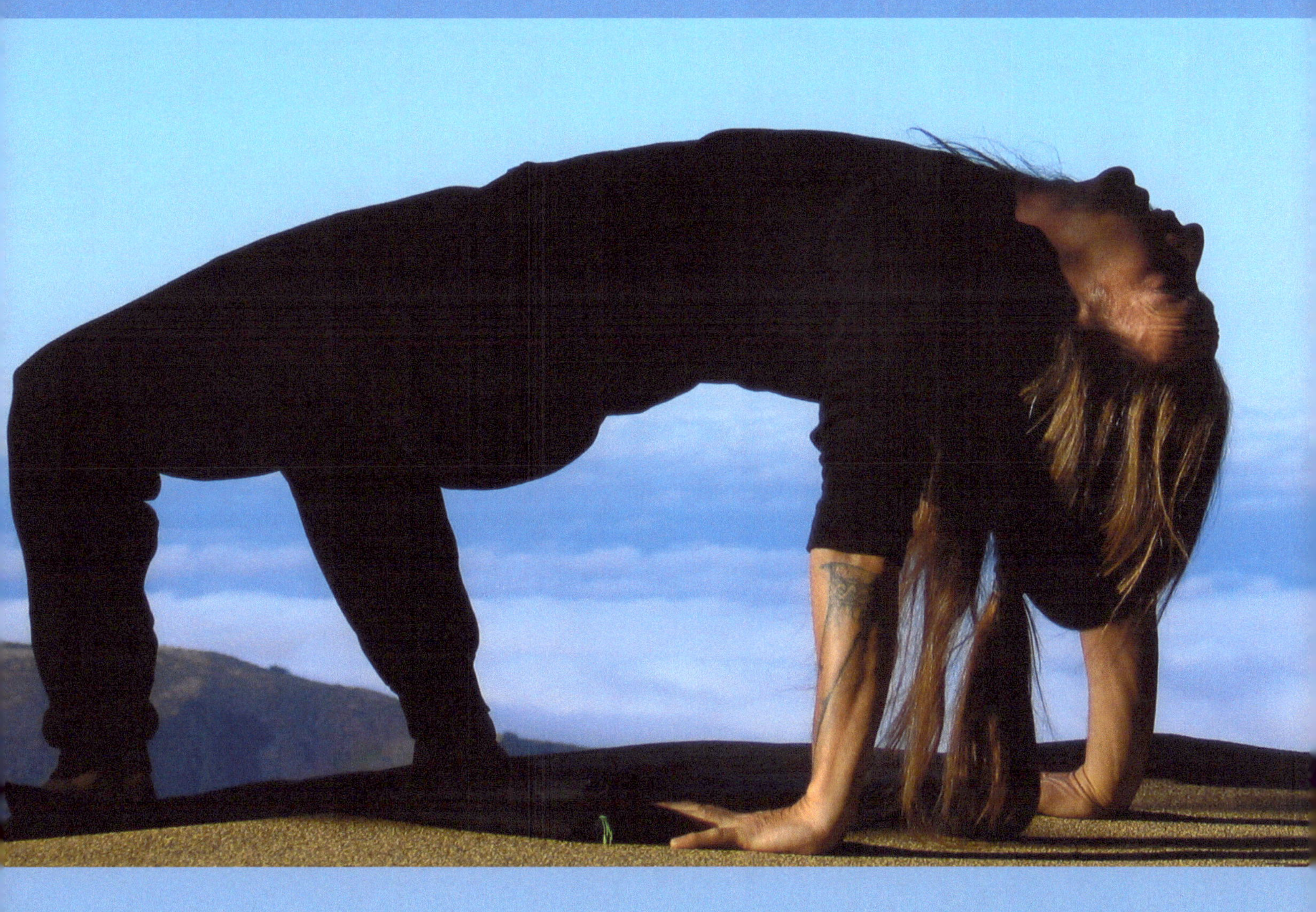

Upward Ox

Upward Ox

*Sitting upright, hands closed, palms down, legs extending,
heels down, toes up.*

*Inhaling, place feet hip width apart, hands shoulder width apart,
rolling shoulders back, raising hips to form table position.
Allow head to fall back comfortably.*

*Exhale, rolling shoulders forward, lowering hips to ground,
extending feet forward, heels to ground, palms facing down,
hands closed.*

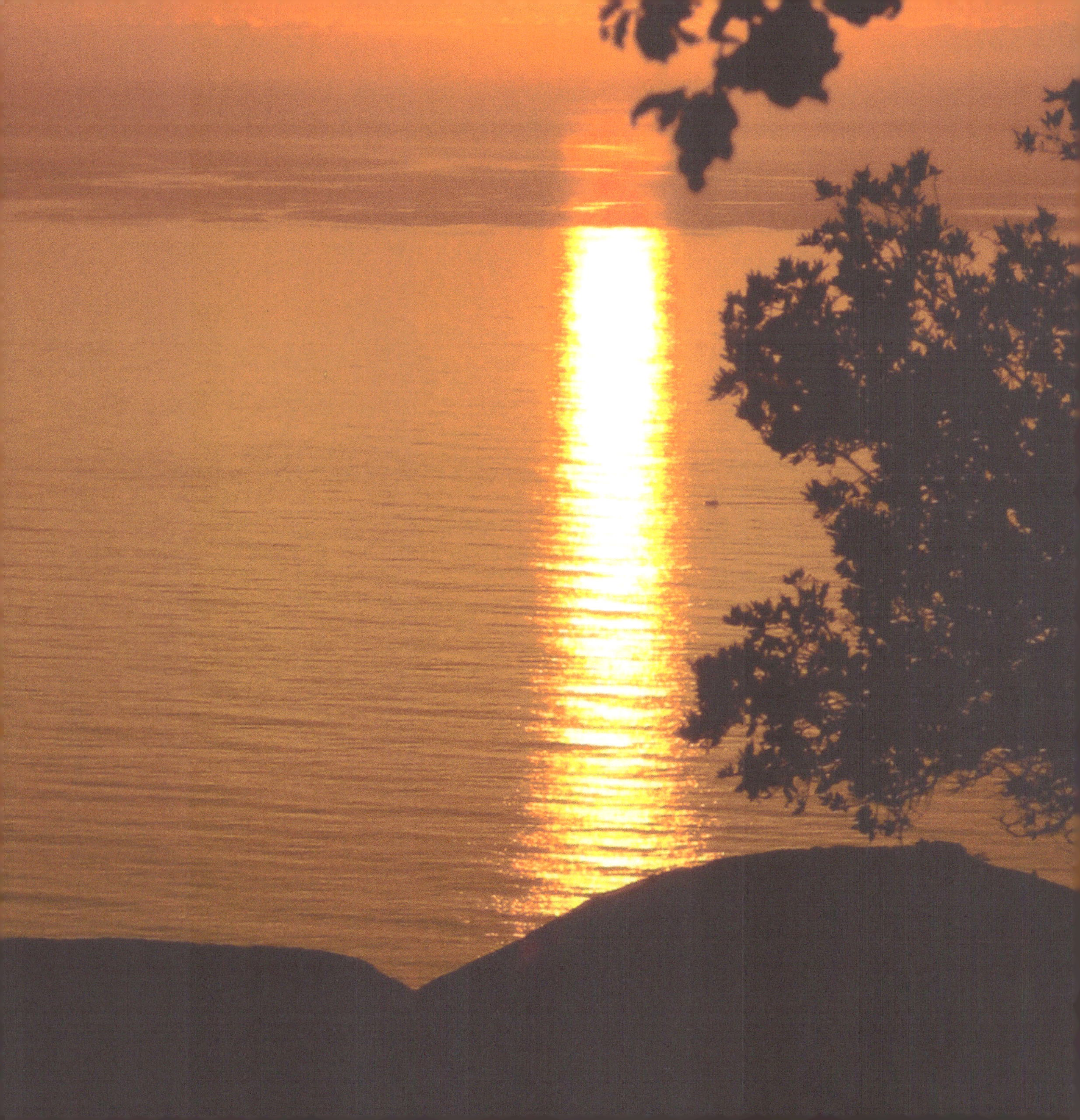

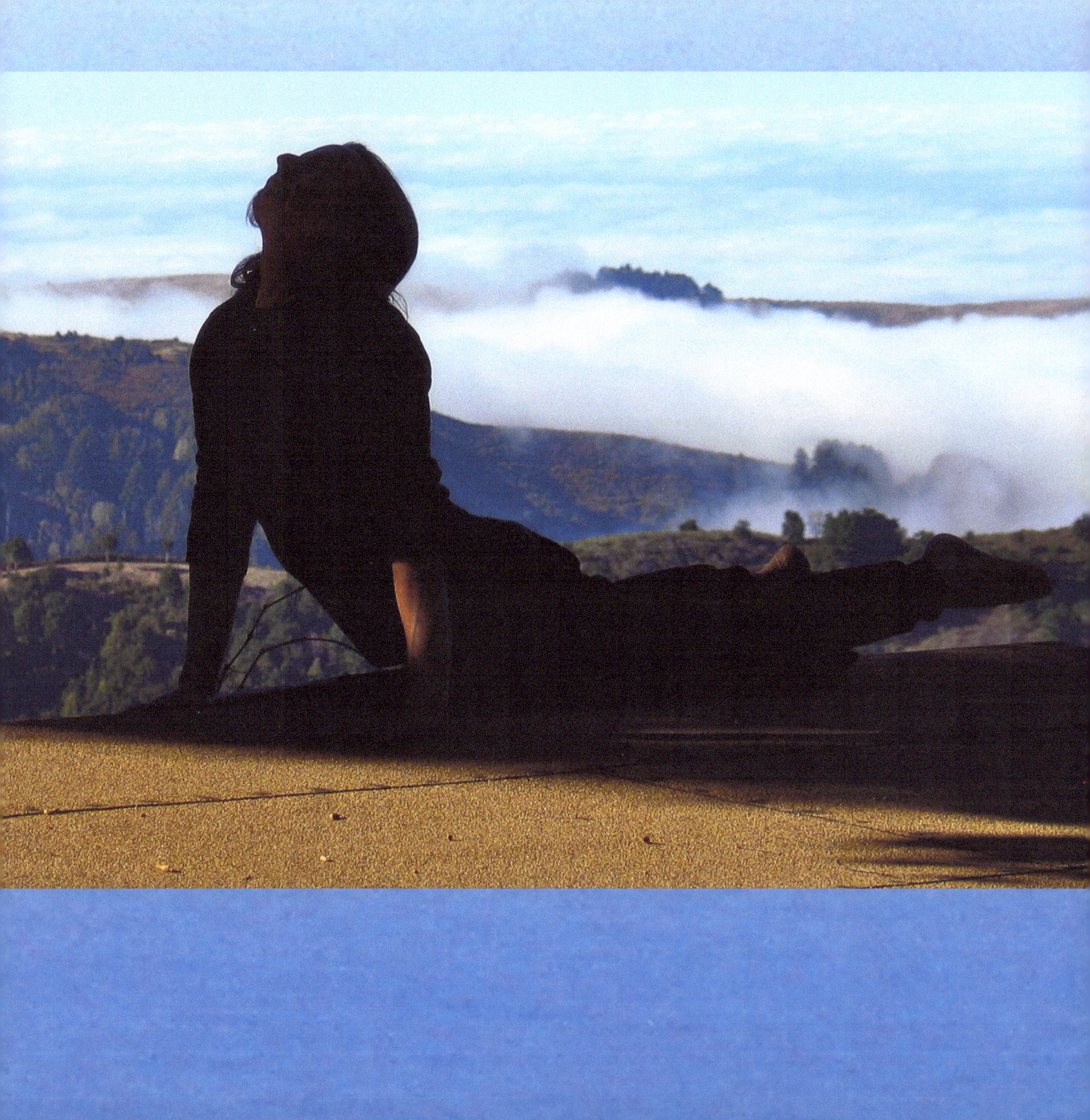

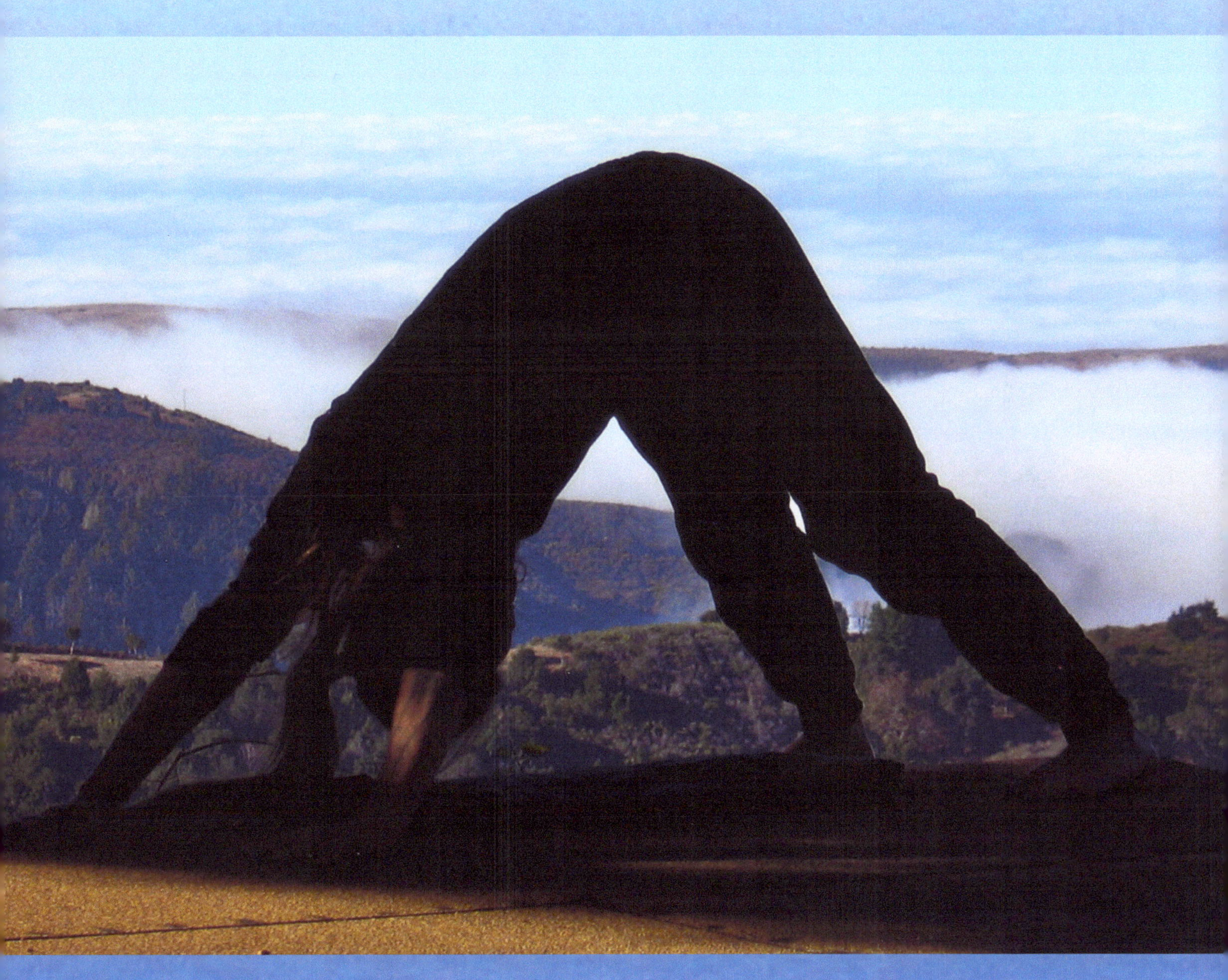

Stretching Dog

Stretching Dog

Lying face down, hands under shoulders, inhaling as
arms straighten, shoulders rolling back, pressing upward,
nose to sky, slightly bending knees, raising feet a few inches.

Exhaling, curling toes forward, placing feet hip width apart,
raising hips skyward, heels reaching toward ground, head
hanging freely between arms.

Inhaling, return.

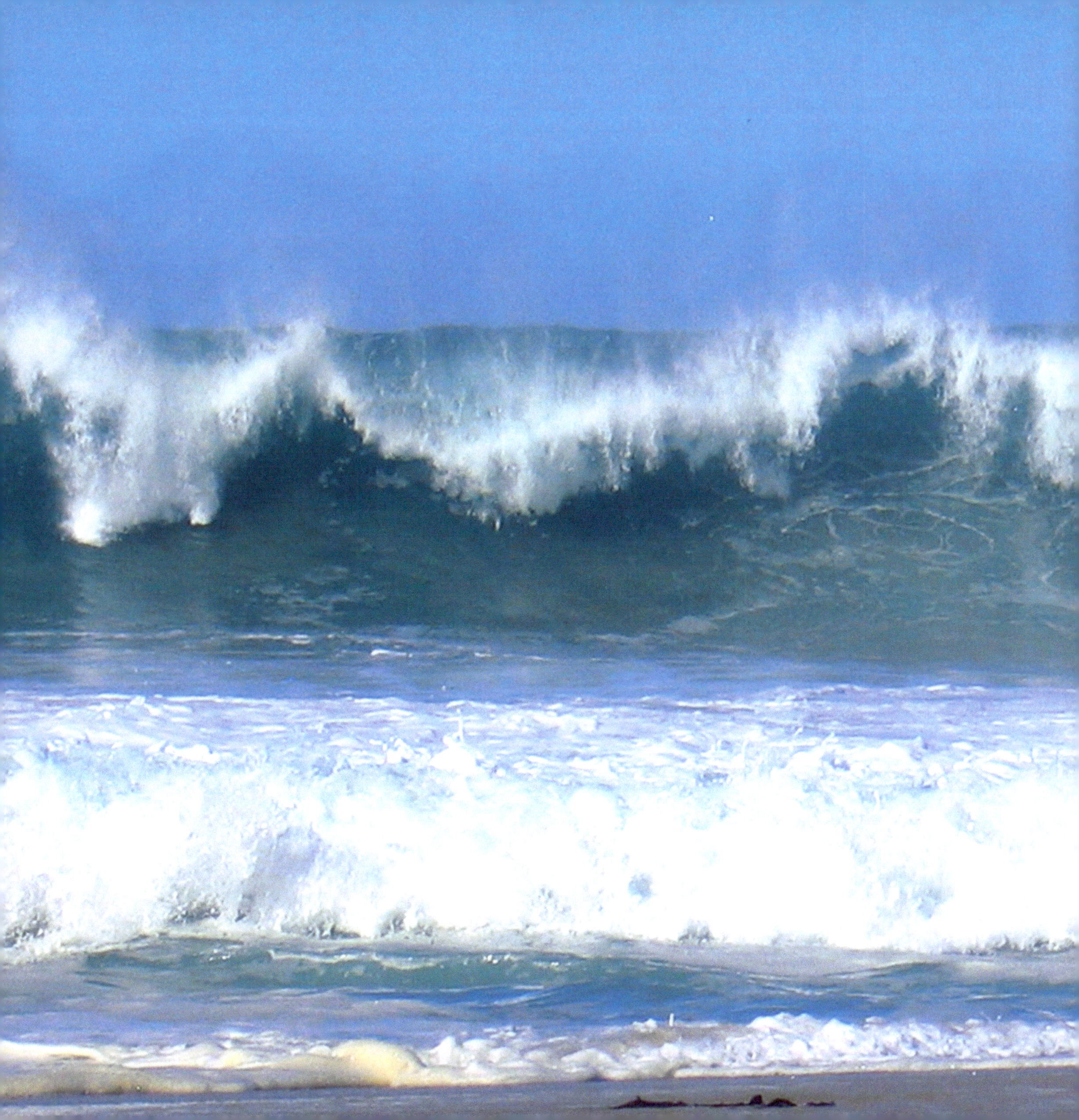

Deeper Still

Enter Spinning / Containing

*Counting revolutions, I turn with complete confidence in where
I am, no dizzy feeling, I know that I will end it well,
and capture all of this energy.*

*Moving clockwise, counter to the earth's movement I see all of my surroundings
from up close to very far away. Rolling my shoulders to stretch my hands wide,
palms up or down in whatever position is pleasing and open,
my feet step lightly as I move.*

*I count to 21, then stop, facing the most pleasing direction.
Bringing both hands together and breathing in, I draw them towards
me, raising elbows, hands together before my face. Breathing out,
I focus on slowly bending my touching knees. Breathing in,
I straighten my knees and raise myself straight up,
pulling taut as a string on a bow.*

*I do this two or three times to contain the effects of twirling and
I am prepared for the next ritual, internally connected and aware of
the self, while externally safe and aware of all my surroundings.*

In between I take three breaths.

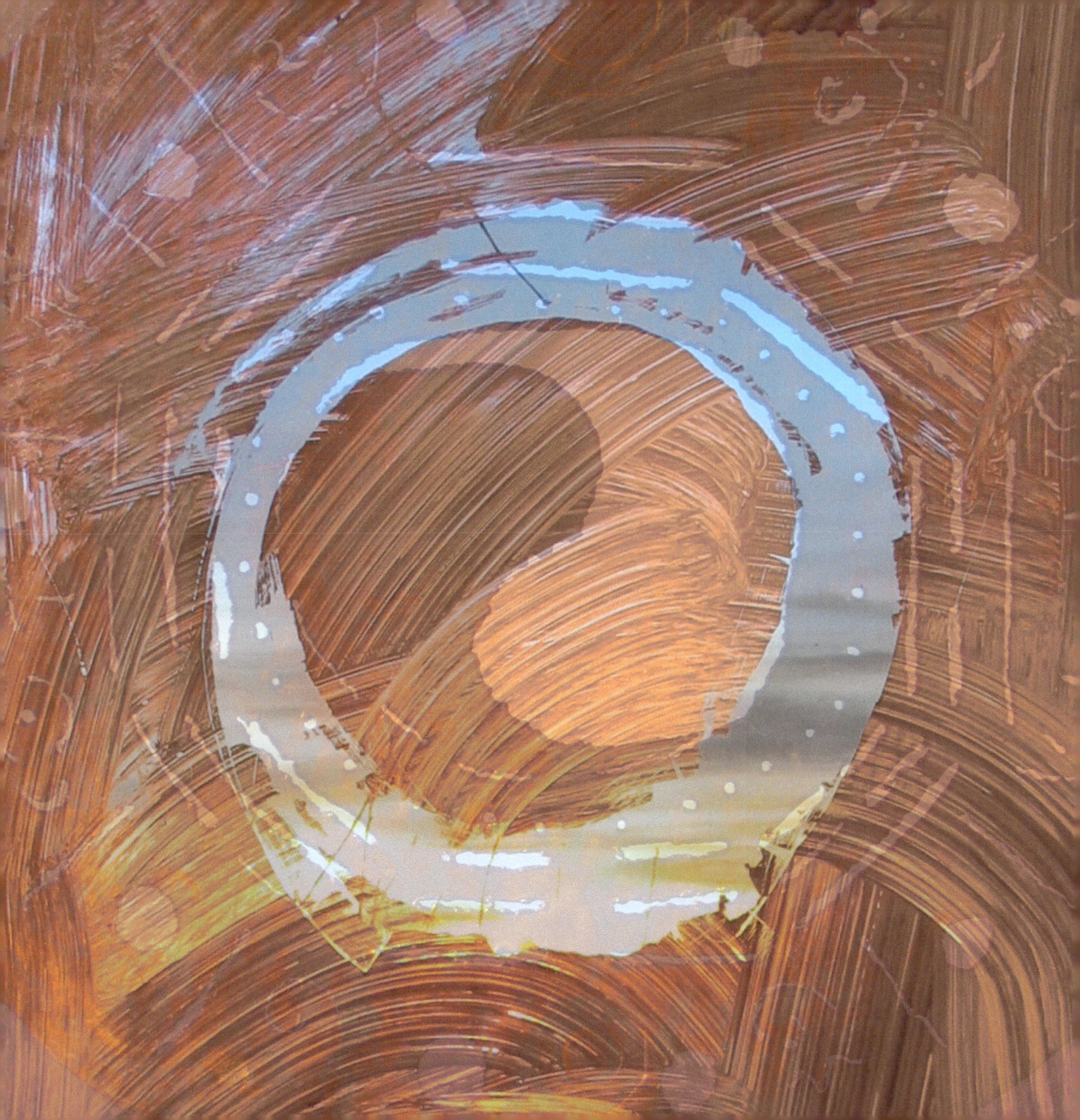

Elevated Soles

I begin flat on my back, arms at my sides, hands closed,
head resting comfortably, heels on the ground. I inhale and roll my
shoulders back, raising my arms and lifting my head, chin towards chest.
At the same time, I raise my feet, lifting my feet straight up towards the sky,
hands held open a few inches above the ground.

I hold for a moment then breathe out,
lowering my feet and head to rest on the ground,
rolling my shoulders back
and closing my hands as they rest, palms down.

I repeat 21 times, keeping my mind focused on the count.

In between I take three breaths.

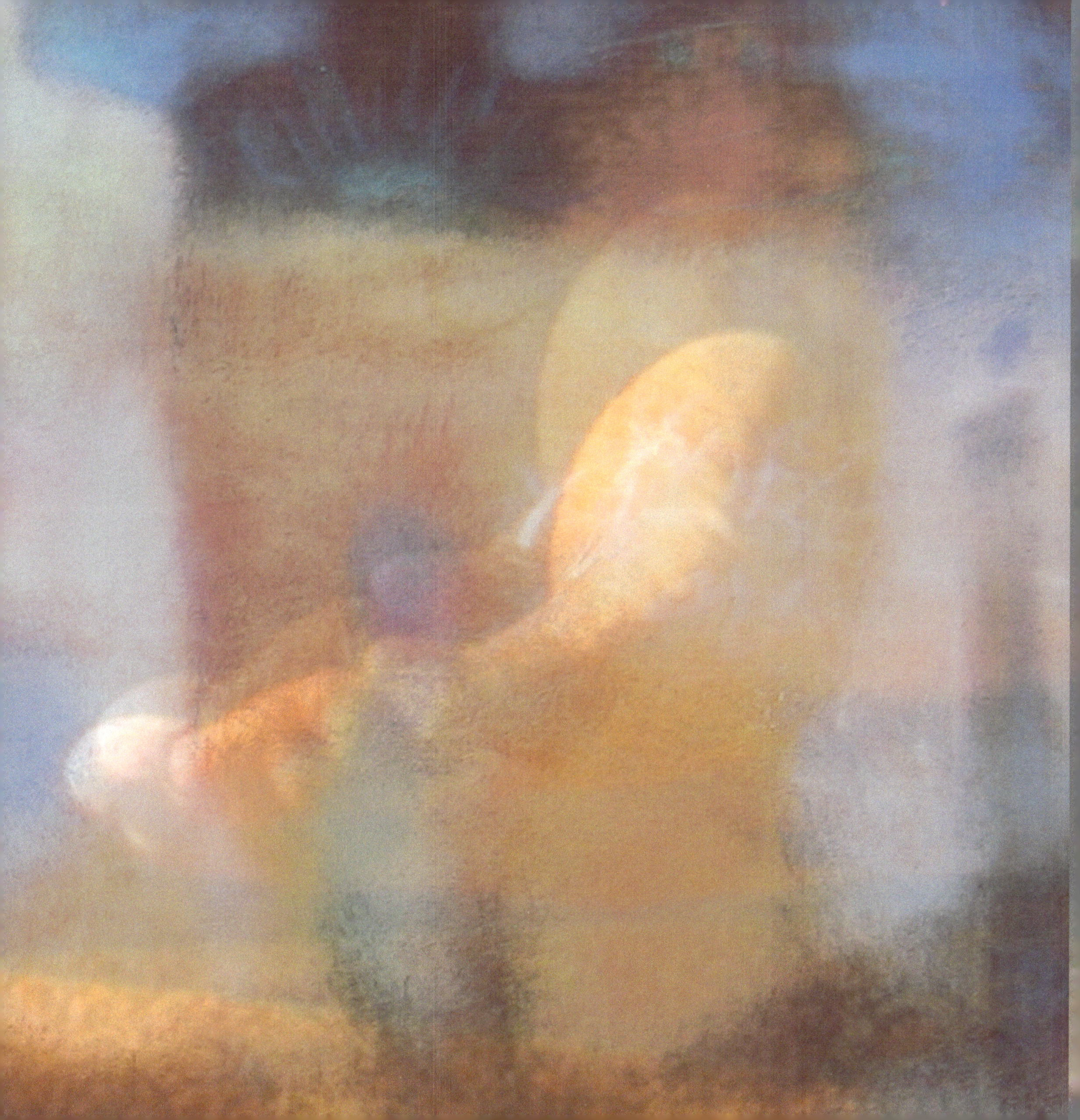

Sunning Roc

I kneel with my weight over my knees, which are hip width apart,
chin toward chest , open hands to sides, arms relaxed
as if filled with sand, palms facing back.

I inhale, rolling shoulders back, allowing chest to expand.
Looking skyward to see as far as my spine and neck allow,
I lean back, chin raised, open hands facing forward.
Weight is pressing tops of feet firmly down.

I hold a moment, then exhale, shoulders rolling forward,
turning palms to face backwards as chin drops to my chest,
weight centered over knees again.

Counting each inhale, careful to stop at 21.

In between I take three breaths.

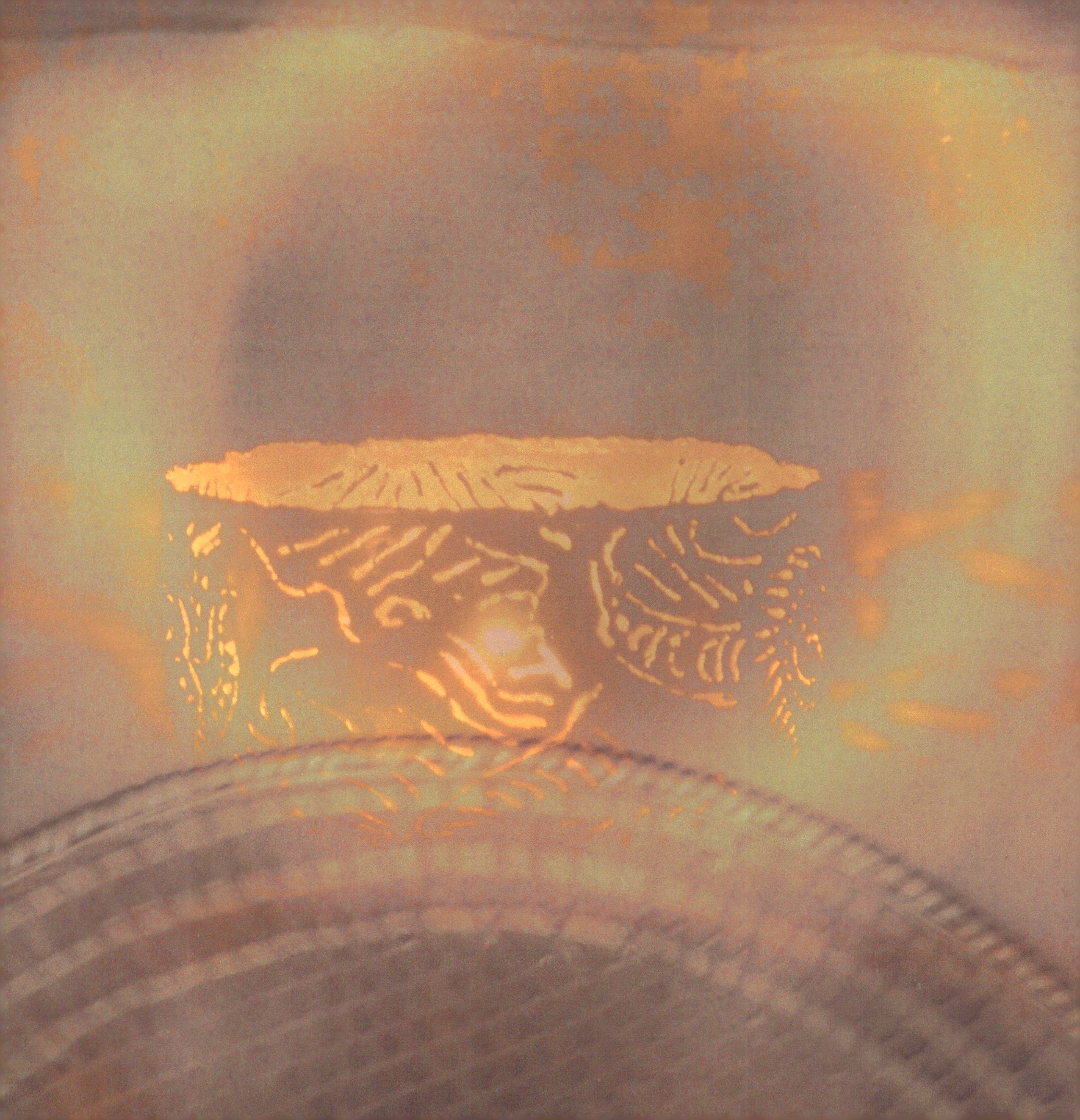

Upward Ox

*I begin sitting, spine straight and legs extended before me,
my hands are closed and off the ground at my sides.*

*I inhale, placing my hands shoulder width apart and feet slightly
wider than hips, I lift myself into the table position.
I allow my head to roll backward comfortably, continuing to
breathe in, pulling abdomen tight.*

*I hold a moment or more,
then exhale, returning seat to ground.
Hands lift to sides, palms closed, and feet again before me,
soles facing forward.*

I remember to breathe and count throughout the ritual.

In between I take three breaths.

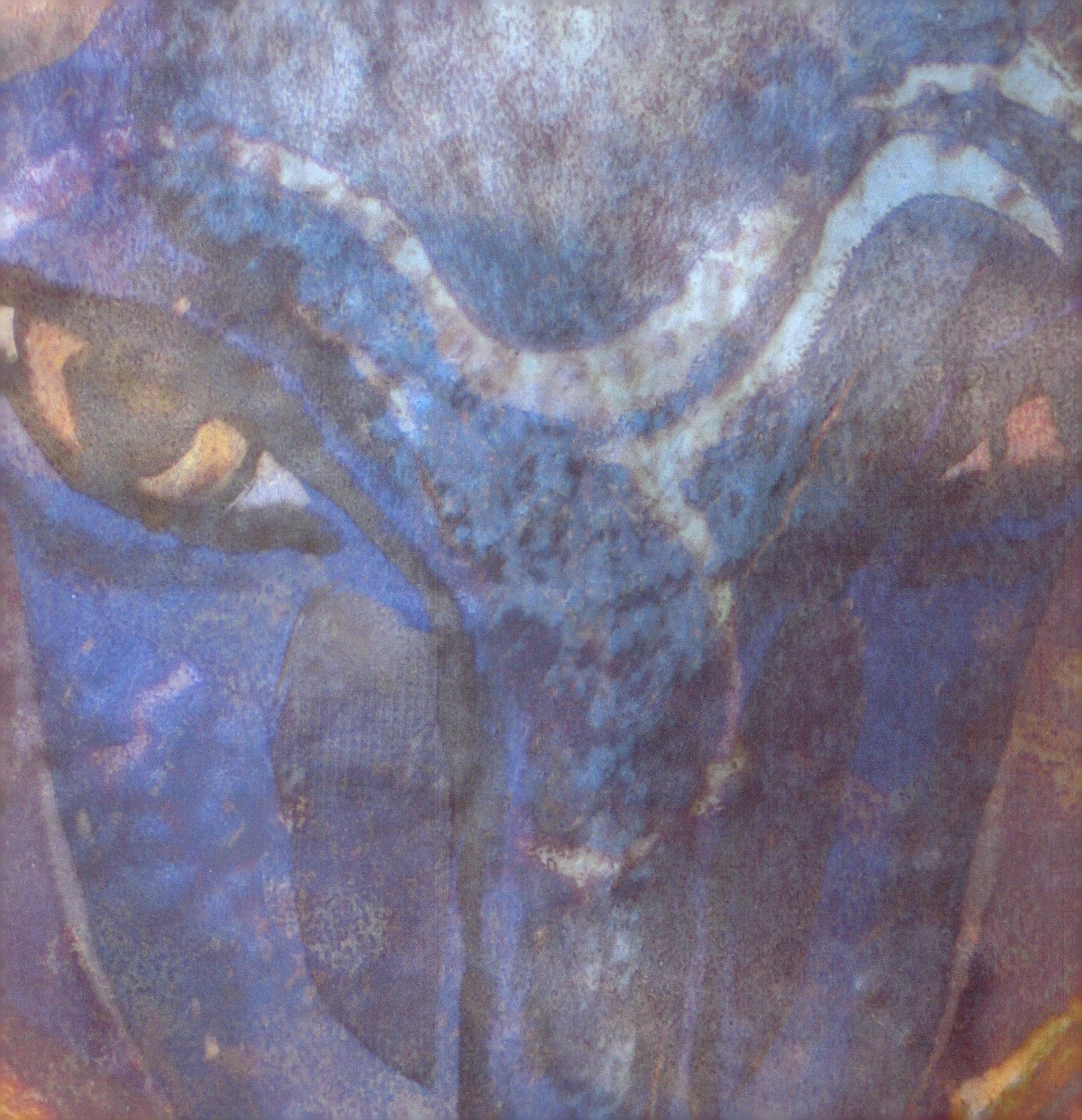

Stretching Dog

I lie down, abdomen to earth, inhaling,
hands beneath shoulders. Feet extended behind me
slightly apart and slightly raised off the ground.

I look forward, lungs expanding as I push my torso upwards.
As I allow my feet to come under me, I exhale, raising tail to sky,
placing feet and hands in a rectangle. I try to plant my heels,
though they might not touch the ground, and allow my head
to drop forward between my arms, chin towards chest,
eyes gazing rearward, restfully inverted.

I exhale as I push forward with my feet and lower my torso
back to the ground.

I remember to count each inhale, and am aware of counting,
knowing I will stop at 21. My mind wants to wander,
but the count is primary, so I count.

.

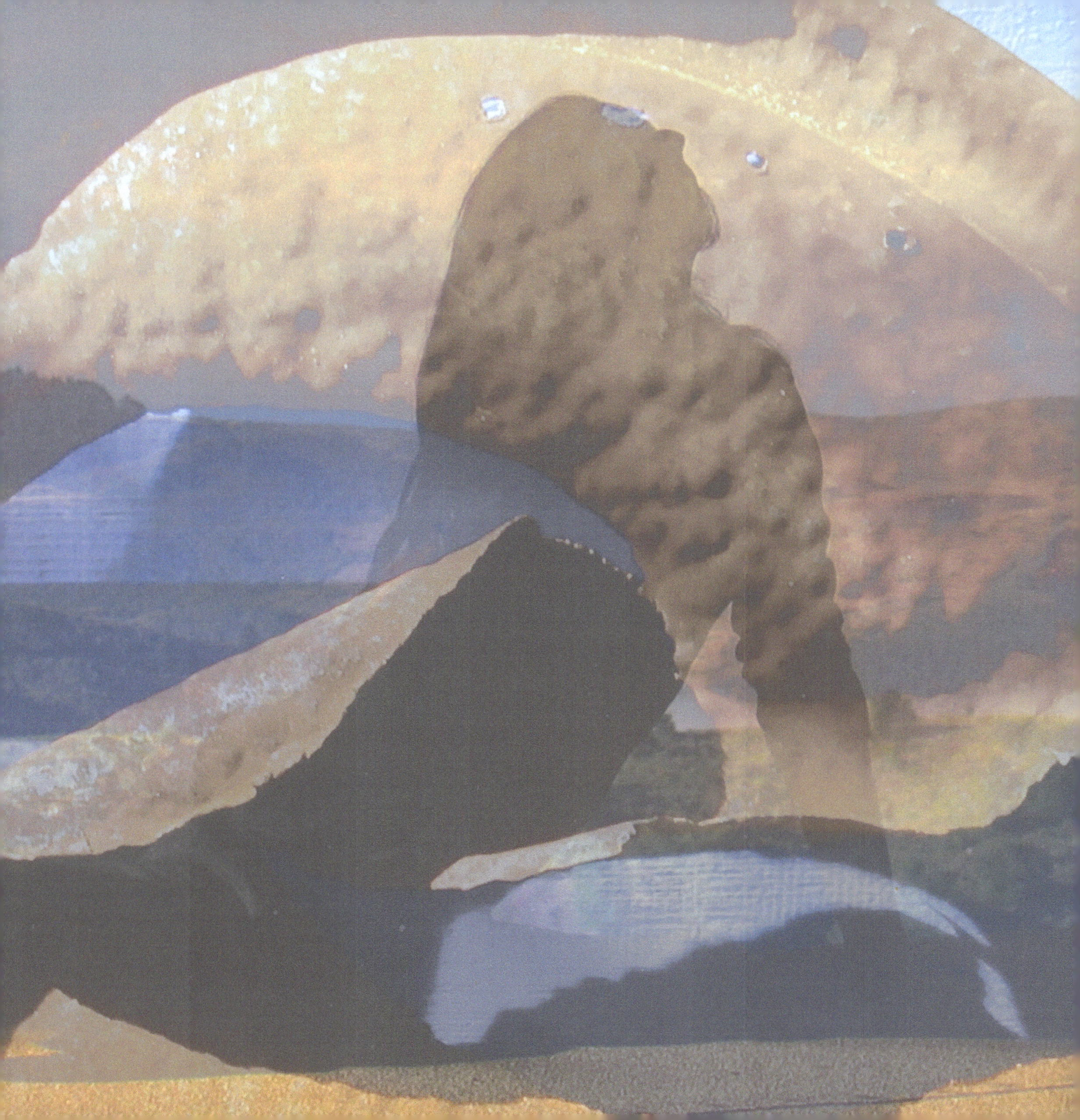

The In Betweens

The In Betweens

*There are four transition spaces in between the 5 Rituals, so I usually face each
of the four corners of my mat or the four directions as I take three or more
breaths: a calming breath, a contemplative breath and a rising breath.
To fully experience each of these may require more than one breath.*

In the calming breath I reel in the energy of the previous ritual.

*In the contemplative breath I contemplate my place at this moment
and set my movement to the next ritual.*

*In the rising breath my energy rises up and I complete
the transition to the next ritual .*

The Count Counts

Keeping count is essential to the ritual, and going past 21 is not necessary.
I was skeptical when I heard this, but it is quite true and will play an important role in
any sincere and earnest practice. In the beginning, start with 5 or so and build up to 21
over time. Eventually, you may need the count to stop yourself from doing more
than 21, and a wandering mind can needlessly overwork the body.

If I lose count, I start at seventeen and do the remaining five counts. Since focus is
always stronger near the end of a ritual, this helps and encourages me.
Also, when I feel injured or weakened for any reason I will start at seventeen to
accommodate temporary limitations. When you are just starting to learn these rituals,
starting the count at seventeen can be helpful.

My experience with counting has been that it is a multidimensional tool
within the rituals. I have found that the count is often a walk through the ages
I have lived. These formative human conditions we all experience in the first 21 years
can cause blockages within our current lives. Practicing the rituals has enabled me to
discover and remove blockages from the past, a fact that has given me
greater emotional and spiritual strength.

I have found that meditation for a short period before the rituals allows me
to perform them with awareness - centered and balanced.
I nearly always do this and recommend it to all.

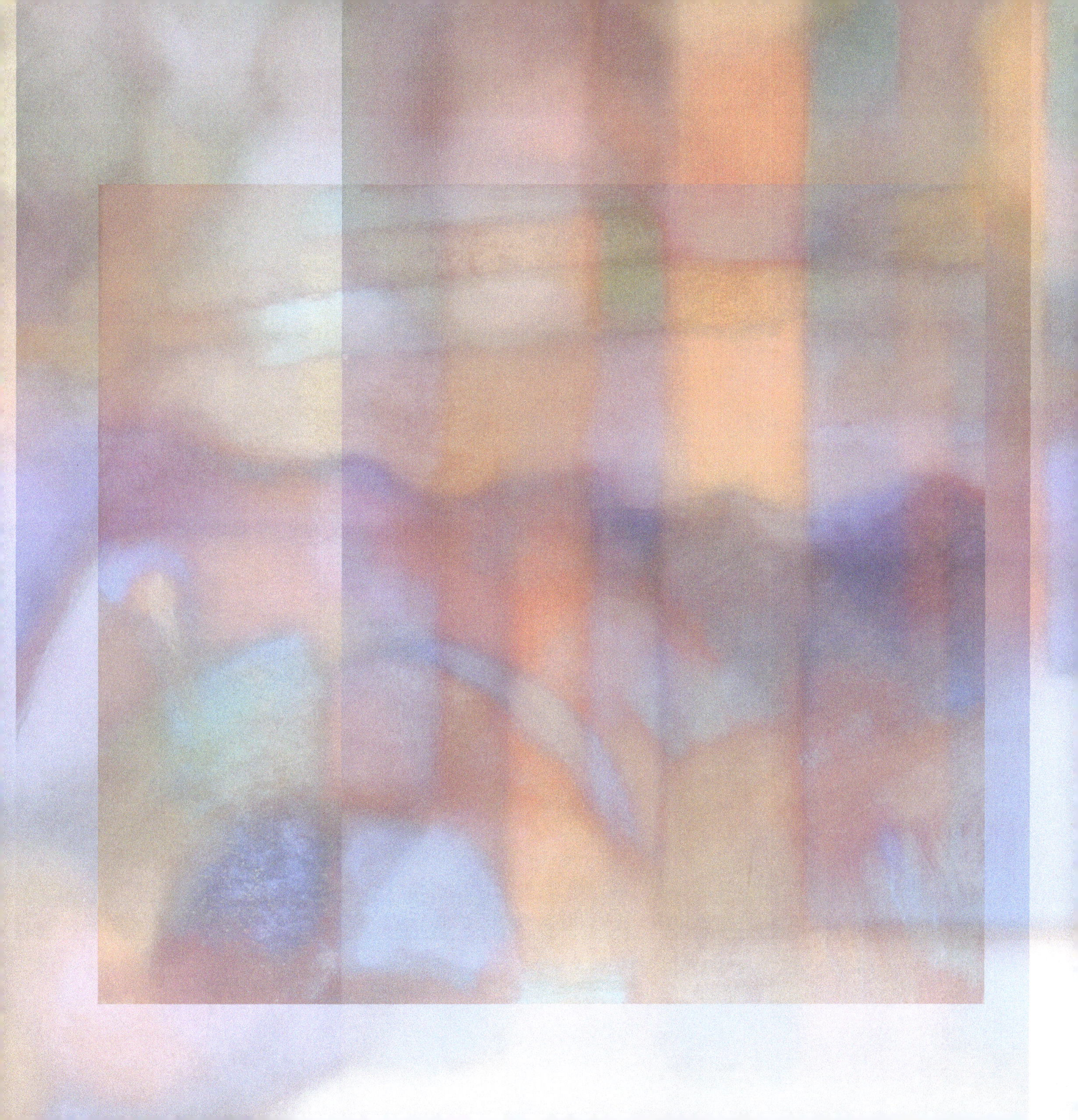

The Speed of Breath

Moving at the "Speed Of Breath" defines the pace of each ritual,
and provides a support rhythm for me, no matter what my current abilities
and condition are. I allow my present state of existence to guide me along
through my practice. Sometimes fast or slow, sometimes long or short,
and sometimes with many breaks, I listen to my body's wisdom.
Muscles and tendons move the bones and joints, all of which are of
miraculous construction, so "they already know the way"!

As above, so below

When I began my practice, I would just focus on the positions of my hands and feet
as I inhaled and exhaled. As I learned, my body instinctively began to guide me
through the movements until they seemed natural. I began to see why the Tibetans
refined and distilled this simple set of movements to be as concise
and completely natural as possible.

 I am grateful for this "whole life" practice, designed to work at all stages of my life, in all
conditions. Whatever obstacles come along, whether physical or situational, the
practice will accommodate me or be adapted to my needs, as it has Tibetans and
others for untold years and in untold conditions. I realize I have one great desire:
that I might awaken next time around, knowing these rituals.

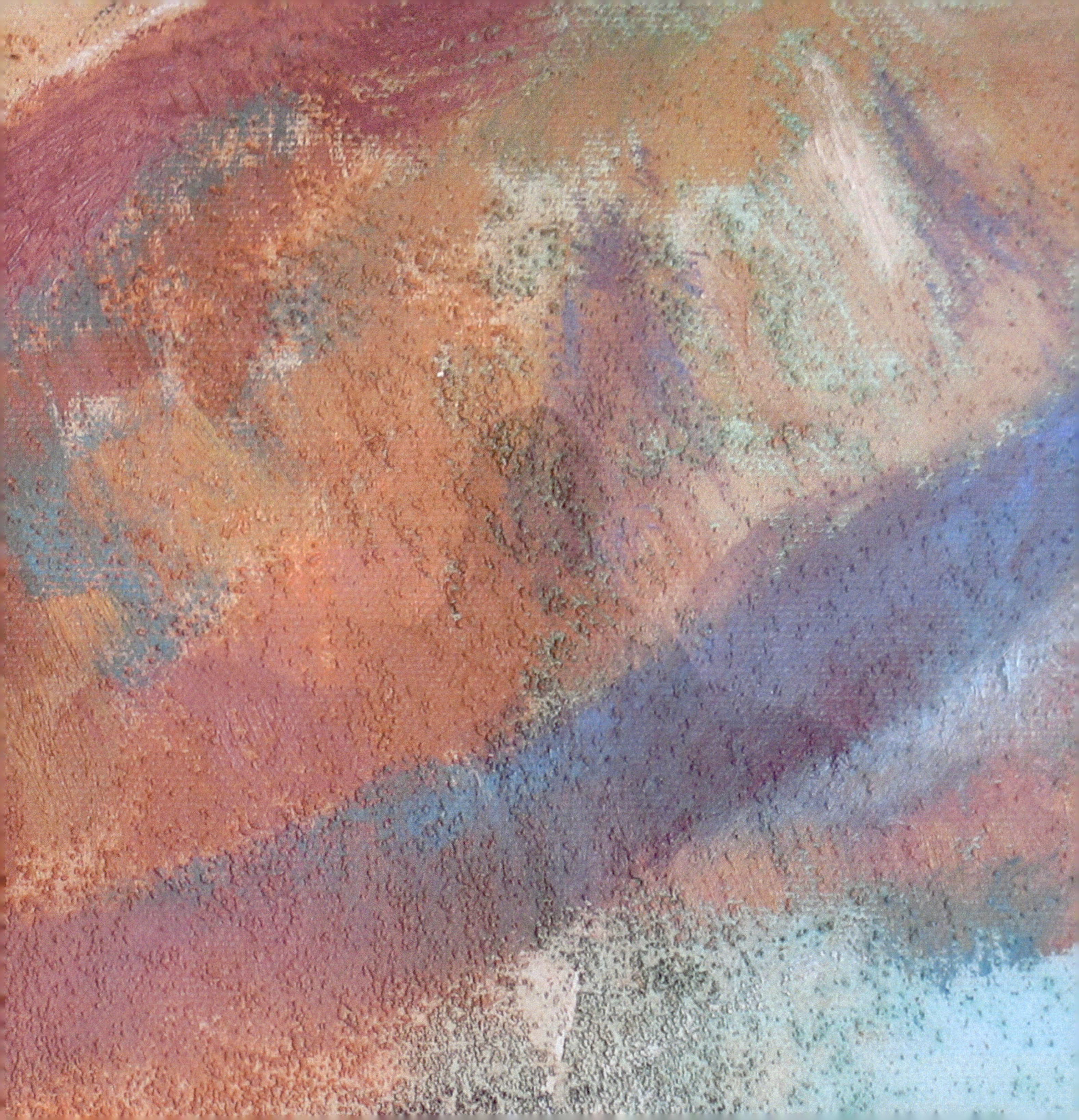

Running Down Hill

When hiking, I enjoy taking advantage of gravity. Sometimes the trail is just too perfect and gravity makes it easier to skip, hop and run. When conditions both within and without myself are "just right" - a ten out of ten - and my perceptions are clear and my concentration unbroken, I run down hill with gravity as an ally.

And then sometimes I follow the conditions, and I simply hike.
And the hike is actually all there is.
The hike offers many things: sights to see and time to think,
contemplation and movement.

The running downhill is something extra, something
you only get a little bit of when things are just right.

I use the same example for doing my T5.
I do the basic movements and ranges of movement required, just
far enough in each position, just long enough at each resting point.

Then sometimes, as conditions become just right, I "run downhill."
I allow myself a bit more stretching range, I inhale and hold
or take two or three breaths as some of the movements allow.
I rotate my joints farther and fuller, I grip the ground with fingers
and toes. I make certain movements a bit straighter and others
I twist and curve a bit further.

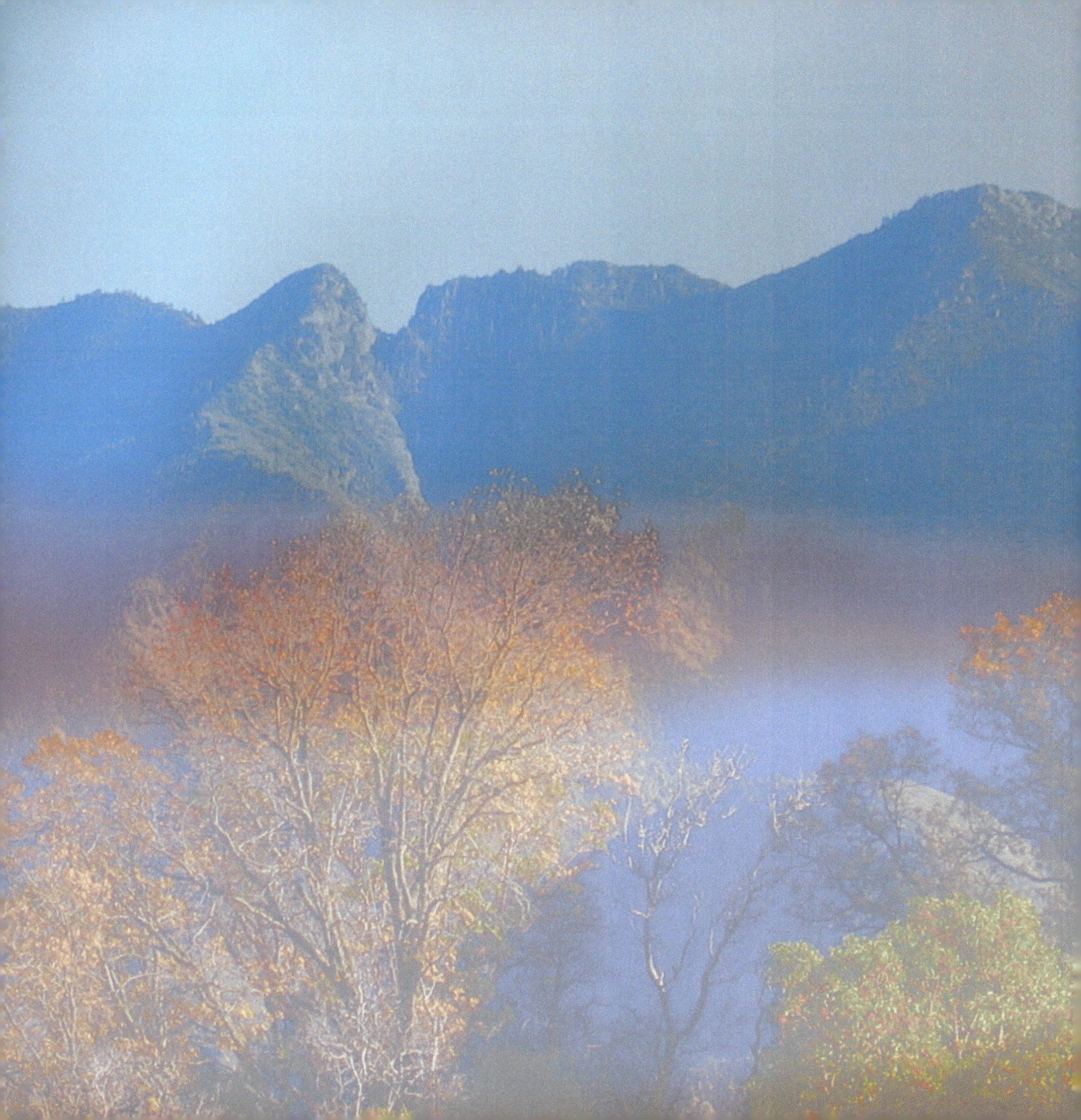

The Differences

 If you have watched on the internet, you have probably seen a dozen or more practices of similar T5 rituals performed. My first exposure to the T5 occurred on a beach in California. A young man had camped with his family in the evening, then in the morning he did his ritual on the beach before they left. It looked really fun, and I knew it was that "Tibetan thing" I had heard about years before but dismissed because I thought the spinning was too weird. At the time, I was sorry I didn't have a chance to chat with the man. A few months later I saw a video online, and started a practice.

MyT5 differs from other practices. The adjustments have evolved as a result of my unique 21st century body responding and making suggestions to the practice. After watching other practitioners, and trying many approaches, I have found that my inner voice says "Yes, that's it!" when I hit on the ways of practicing that benefit and suit me the most. In the past, if I've resisted hearing that voice, I always eventually come around to the wisdom of its way. I practice as though I always have and always will.

I am grateful for the conditions of my path during the time I was developing this practice. I had retired into a personal hermitage, so for over six years I had the opportunity to devote much time, discipline and contemplation to its evolution. This book is a distillation which I offer to those who might not have the kind of time or situation required to develop their own practice, yet want to learn a simple, time-honored one to start with. In the end, everyone develops their own way of practicing the T5. Our bodies are as different as they are the same and the T5 is a transitional device, made up entirely of transitions. So it is perfectly natural for us all to have our own T5 since we are all in a natural state of transition.

When and Where to Practice

While ideal locations, conditions and times exist, it is THAT I practice which is important. I always try to go outdoors, even if I have to get bundled up, but the T5 isn't meant to be a struggle. As countless Tibetans have been held under harsh conditions, I could imagine this practice taking place in prison cells and work camps, very likely covertly. So wherever I am able to practice, I do.

Ideally, practice somewhere beautiful, somewhere "sacred" and where there is fresh air and a clean space or mat. An open, expansive view is nice. The long horizontal shadows of daybreak and evening remind me of the passing of time. Vertical lines both front and back are convenient markers for aligning myself during practice. I don't go looking for these things - they seem to reveal themselves as I settle into the practice and a part of me allows my awareness to grow. I feel protected by this part of who I am. Insects or other distractions can occur, but the counting and steady breathing keep me focussed on my practice.

When to practice is going to be up to you, but should be what is most easy for you to maintain. I have had periods where I practiced daily for months (that is "running downhill"). The most effective pattern I have found is to practice 5 of every 7 days: 3 days in a row, skip a day and then 2 days in a row. The defining moment comes when perhaps a couple of weeks have passed with no practicing, and I say to myself "Today I practice, or I have no practice at all".

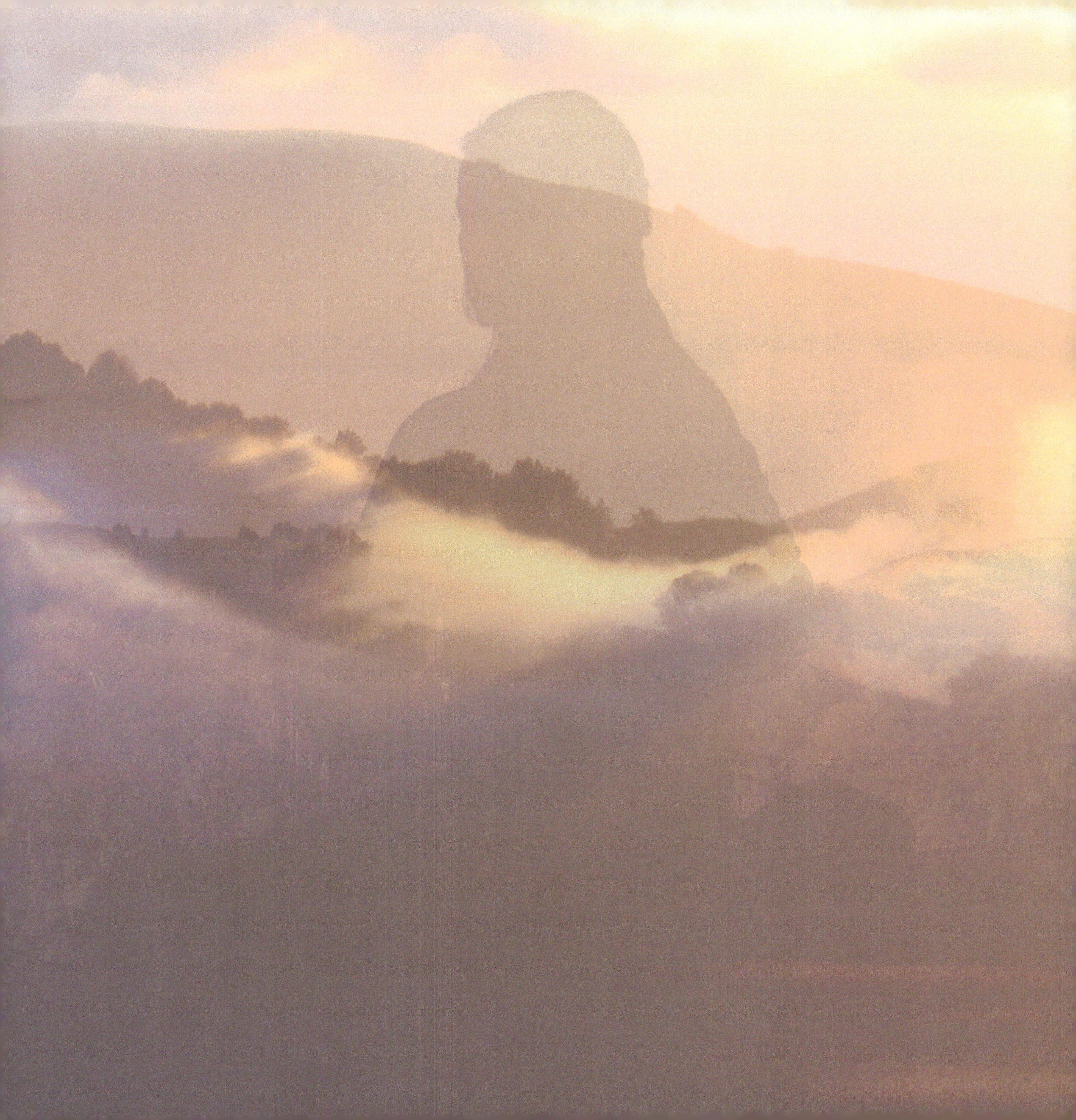

Who I am protects me

*We are all learning ways to protect ourselves from things in our environment
which may not be beneficial to us. There is a level of self-trust which shouldn't
be taken for granted. In myT5 I have learned how much this trust reaches into
my own life and how I am able to see its effects all around me in all I do.
Most of us are in need of improvement, and beginning a sincere and
practical discipline of our own can be a first step on the path to getting better.
Your practice is fundamental and is enough, but we must all be able to survive the
elements (be that a home or a cave) and to feed ourselves. These are basic forms
of self-protection, but they are not who you are. You are not any of your things or
the people in your life, however much they may protect you.
But a sincere practice in your life will protect you and is you.*

Immortality

*Living immortally is a real and true possibility, it's nothing complicated. It is obvious
yet widely overlooked and misunderstood. There is much confusion around the idea
of living forever and most don't believe in immortality, let alone practice it.
Simply put, immortality is this:
Do not allow another to kill you, and do not take part in killing yourself.*

*Living each moment with that truth is all we can ask for,
and in most cases is likely to lead to a next moment. Living in such a moment
is truly living: from this moment to the next. Until you don't!*

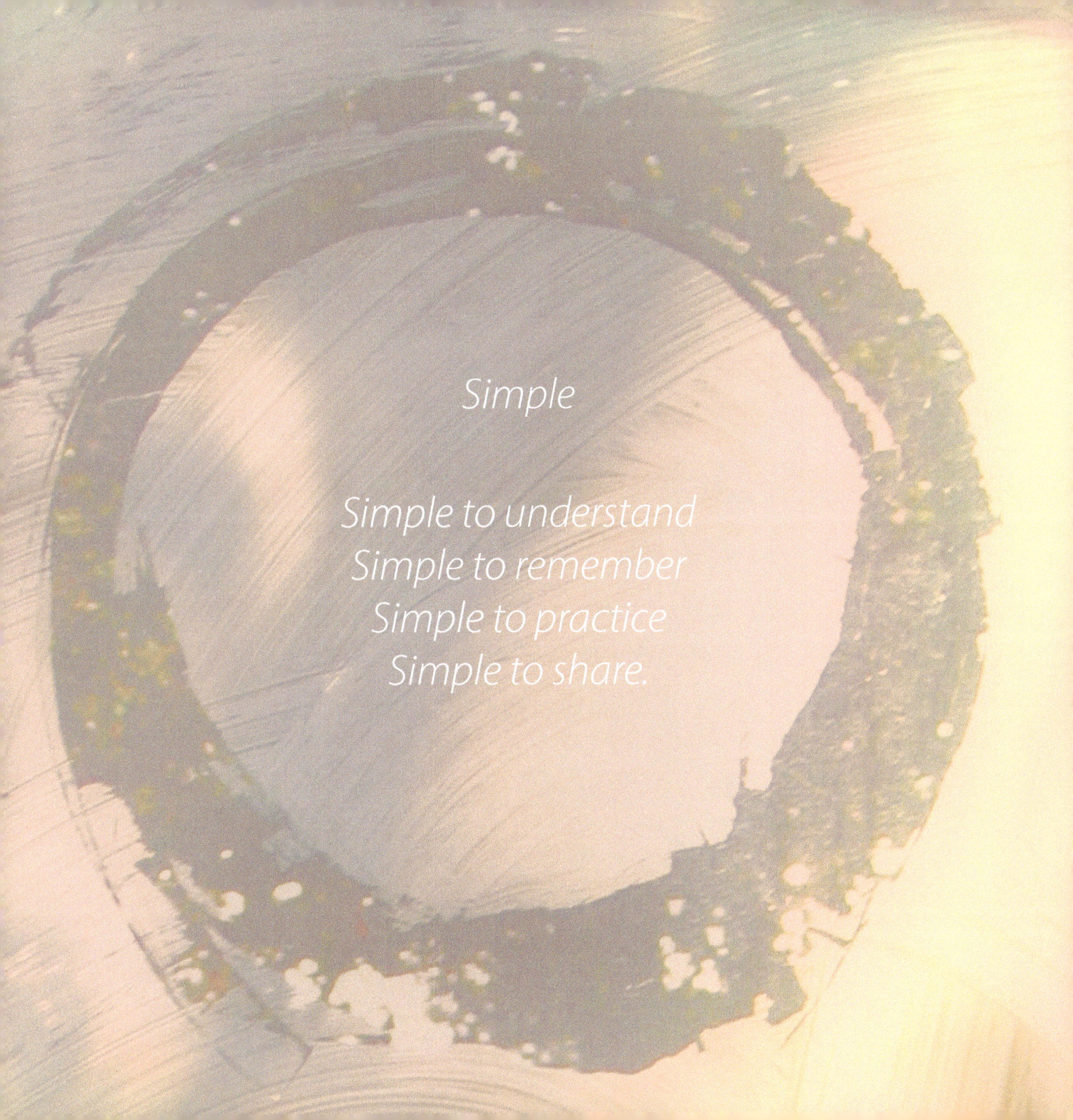
Simple

Simple to understand
Simple to remember
Simple to practice
Simple to share.

Writing this book has been a longtime desire of Jesse's. I am very happy to have been a co-creating, brainstorming part of its conception and birth. Jesse's generous spirit shines through every page. May his message shine through with clarity and inspire all who encounter it!

— Melissa Lofton

Melissa Lofton has poured heart and soul into this book, surrounding the reader with an abundance of evocative imagery, which gently guides through a journey of discovering the 5 Tibetan rituals. Words are only the framework of real communication. What she has provided scores and choreographs the true message of the T5. I am grateful beyond words for her partnership in this book.

— Jesse Hamilton V

Our tremendous gratitude goes to David and Ginna Gordon of Lucky Valley Press for their continual support, advice, editing, hand holding, encouragement, enthusiasm and, most of all, friendship throughout the process of publishing this book.

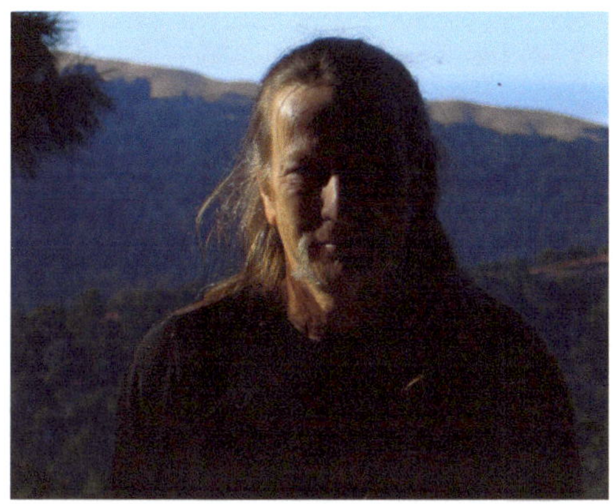

Having spent years practicing martial arts and Eastern studies, author Jesse Hamilton has developed a unique, individual practice of the 5Tibetan rituals, a highly effective and accessible system to strengthen body, mind and spirit. In this book he shares with you the essentials of this ancient practice to aid you in developing a practice of your own.
In addition to cultivating a daily practice, Hamilton is a sculptor working with metal and light. His work can be seen on his website: www.oxendragon.com

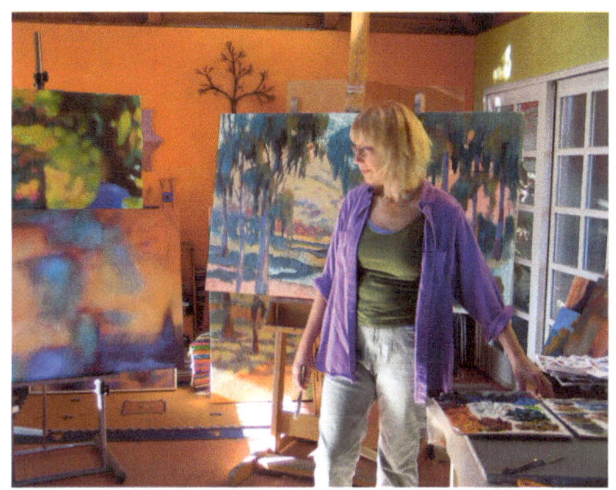

Artist Melissa Lofton, who is well known for her paintings in oil, has been photographing images from nature and people and from her lifetime of living in the Big Sur CA area. In designing this book, she draws from these images, overlaid with details of her paintings as well as images of Jesse's metal work. More of her work can be seen on the website: www.mlofton.com
Photograph: Debi Lorenc

My T5
Text © 2017 Jesse Hamilton
All rights reserved

Images © 2017 Melissa Lofton
All rights reserved

Book design by Melissa Lofton

All images in this book are photographs
and/or details of paintings by Melissa Lofton

ISBN: 978-0-692-84068-9

Published by Oxendragon Press
PO Box 223634
Carmel, California 93922

Prepress by LuckyValley Press
Jacksonville, Oregon 97530